A Guide to

I·R·I·S·H

CHURCHES AND
GRAVEYARDS

A Guide to

I·R·I·S·H
CHURCHES AND
GRAVEYARDS

Compiled Under the Direction of
Brian Mitchell

Genealogical Publishing Co., Inc.

INTRODUCTION

This book attempts to identify the location of all churches and graveyards in every county of Ireland. The source of this information has lain for over one hundred years within the pages of the Griffith's or Primary Valuation of Ireland. This survey, in which every head of household in Ireland was recorded, was carried out under the direction of Sir Richard Griffith between 1848 and 1864. All churches and graveyards were listed in this survey, but until now this information has remained "buried" among the listings of one million heads of household.

The value of church registers and gravestone inscriptions is self-evident to the family historian. Civil registration of births, deaths, and Roman Catholic marriages begins in 1864 and of Protestant marriages in 1845. Before this period church registers may provide the only reference to an ancestor's birth, marriage or death. However, owing to the destruction of many Church of Ireland burial records and the late commencement dates of so many Roman Catholic and Presbyterian burial registers, a gravestone inscription may be the only record of an ancestor's death. But bear in mind that gravestones offer more than just a mere date of death. They frequently mention a person's residence and his age at death, thus providing an approximate birthdate. Many graves are family plots and the gravestone will record the deaths of other family members.

In this book, each church, including its denomination, is identified against a townland or street address and an Ordnance Survey map number. (With the Ordnance Survey number the exact location of the church can be identified on the six-inch Ordnance Survey map.) Each townland or street is located within its appropriate civil parish, and each civil parish is listed in alphabetical order within its county and is preceded by a number which gives its location in *A New Genealogical Atlas of Ireland* by Brian Mitchell (Genealogical Publishing Company, 1986).

On extracting a list of those churches of interest to you, i.e. usually the ones closest to the townland and/or parish your ancestor lived in, the next step is to determine which registers survive and where they can be found. The *Guide to Irish Parish Registers* by Brian Mitchell (Genealogical Publishing Company, 1988) attempts to do this, as it lists on a civil parish basis the surviving pre-1870 church registers together with their earliest commencement dates.

Also with this book the quick identification of all relevant graveyards is now very feasible. All burial grounds are identified against their townland within the appropriate civil parish and county. The general location of the graveyard within its civil parish can be identified in *A New Genealogical Atlas of Ireland,* while the Ordnance Survey six-inch map will pinpoint its exact location. With the establishment of new churches throughout the nineteenth century, many graveyards attached to the old church fell into disuse and can be easily overlooked. For example, the original Church of Ireland burial ground for Desertoghill Parish, Co. Londonderry, now lies one mile to the north of the new church and graveyard. There is now no trace of the original parish church, and the old burial ground is set back from the road and hidden by a dry-stone wall and hedgerows. Only by stumbling on a person with good local knowledge would a visitor identify this graveyard. This book, however, identifies all graveyards, including those which have long been separated from any church in use today. In nearly every case a graveyard on its own will identify the location of a former church.

If the graveyard symbol is entered on the same line as the church symbol then the graveyard is attached to that church. Generally, Church of Ireland graveyards should be examined irrespective of an ancestor's religion. It was October 1829 before a Catholic cemetery opened in Dublin at Goldenbridge. Prior to the 1820s, owing to the operation of the Penal Laws, both Catholics and Protestants shared the same graveyards. And prior to the Burial Act of 1868, which permitted dissenting ministers to conduct burial services, the Church of Ireland clergy held jurisdiction over funeral services for all Protestants. Right up to the mid-nineteenth century it is not uncommon to find Presbyterian ministers and Methodist preachers buried in a Church of Ireland cemetery.

ACKNOWLEDGEMENTS

Many thanks to Ann Doherty, Gail Johnston, Mark McLaughlin and Paul McLoone who extracted the information from the Griffiths Valuation. Michael McLaughlin, Niamh O'Sullivan and Norman Surko checked through the transcribed work sheets. The church and graveyard listings were tabulated by Mark McLaughlin and Paul McLoone and typed by Hillary Neely and Moira Williamson. All are on the staff of the Inner City Trust, Londonderry. Funding of the project was made possible by the Northern Ireland Department of Economic Development.

Brian Mitchell

KEY

The sequence followed in this book for each civil parish is as follows:

1. The number preceding the civil parish represents the map reference number used in *A New Genealogical Atlas of Ireland*.
2. The name of the civil parish in alphabetical order within county.
3. The name of the townland or town and street in which a church or graveyard was located in the mid-nineteenth century.
4. The number following the townland is the Ordnance Survey sheet number in which the townland can be located.
5. In the church column are identified the chapels, meeting houses and churches of the various denominations. The symbols used to denote religious denominations are listed on a separate page.
6. In the graveyard column are identified all graveyards, burial grounds or cemeteries. If the graveyard symbol is on the same line as the church symbol then the graveyard is attached to that church.

Religious Denominations

Church of Ireland or Established Church	EC
Presbyterian Meeting House	P
Roman Catholic Chapel	RC
Seceder's Presbyterian Meeting House	SP
Reformed Presbyterian Meeting House	RP
Methodist Meeting House (Wesleyan or Primitive Wesleyan)	M
Covenanter's Meeting House	COV
Baptist Meeting House	BAP
Congregational Church	CON
Moravian Chapel	MO
Society of Friends Meeting House (i.e. Quakers)	Q
Independent Meeting House	I
Unitarian Meeting House	U
Christian Brethren's Meeting House	CB
Arian Meeting House	A
Bethesda Chapel	BA
Bethel Chapel	BL
Calvinist Meeting House	CAL
Crotty's Meeting House	CY
Darbyite Meeting House	D
Ebenezer Chapel	EZ
Jewish Synagogue	J
Remonstrant Presbyterian Meeting House	REM
Union Prayer Meeting House	UP
Zion Chapel	Z

COUNTY ANTRIM

NGA No.	CIVIL PARISH	TOWNLAND OR TOWN, STREET	OS No.	CHURCH	GRAVE-YARD
1	Aghagallon	Aghagallon	62,66		G
		Ballymacilrany	62	M	
		Derrymore	62		G
		Derrynaseer	66	RC	
2	Aghalee	Aghalee	62,63 66		G
		Poobles	66,67	EC	
3	Ahoghill	Village of Ahoghill	37	P	G
				EC	G
		Gloonan	37	P	G
		Village of Gracehill	37	MO	
					G
		Lismurnaghan	37	P	G
				RC	G
4	Antrim	Antrim, Ferguson's Entry	50	M	
		Main Street		P	
				EC	G
		Scotch Quarter		M	
				Ruins of P	
				U	
		Kilbegs	49,50		G
		Townparks	50	RC	
5	Ardclinis	Town of Carnlough	25	M	
		Carrivemurphy	20	RC	G
		Lemnalary	25	EC	G
		Nappan	20,25		G
6	Armoy	Cromaghs	13	RC	
		Glebe	13	EC	G
		Moyaver Lower	13	P	G
7	Ballinderry	Aghacarnan	63	P	G
		Ballinderry	62,63		G
				MO	G
		Ballykelly	63	Old EC	G

1

NGA No.	CIVIL PARISH	TOWNLAND OR TOWN, STREET	OS No.	CHURCH	GRAVE- YARD
7	Ballinderry	Ballyscolly	63	EC	
		Templecormac	63		G
		Tullyballydonnell	62,63	RC	
8	Ballintoy	Araboy	3,7	P	
		Ballinlea Lower	8	RC	
		Ballintoy Demesne	4	EC	G
		Templastragh	3		G
		Toberkeagh	7,8	P	
9	Ballyclug	Ballylesson	37,38		G
		Ballymarlagh	37,38	EC	G
		Crebilly	32,33, 38	RC	G
10	Ballycor	Ballycor	45		G
		Ballyeaston	45	P	
		Village of Ballyeaston	45	EC P	G
11	Ballylinny	Ballylinny	54	P	G G
		Kingsbog	51	P	
12	Ballymartin	Ballymartin	51		G
13	Ballymoney	Ballymoney, Castle Street	17	RC	G
		Charles Street		U	
		Charlotte Street		COV	G
		Church Street		EC	G
		Meeting House Lane		P	
		Rodden Foot Street		P	
		Carryduff	17,22	P	
		Drumreagh	16,17	P	G
		Roseyards	12	P	
		Townparks	17	P	
14	Ballynure	Town of Ballyclare, Townfoot	45	M	
		Town of Ballynure	45	P M	

2

NGA No.	CIVIL PARISH	TOWNLAND OR TOWN, STREET	OS No.	CHURCH	GRAVE-YARD
14	Ballynure	Village of Straid	46	P	
		Toberdowney	45	EC	G
15	Ballyrashane	Ballywatt Leggs	6	P	
16	Ballyscullion	Ballyscullion East	36,42	RC	
17	Ballywillin	Glebe	3		G
		Portrush, Bushmills Road	2	M	
				RC	
		Main Street		P	
				EC	
18	Belfast	See BELFAST CITY			
19	Billy	Bushmills, Main Street	37	M	
				P	
		Meeting House Lane		P	
		Cabragh or Cavanmore	7	P	
		Glebe	7	EC	G
		Lisnagunogue Lower	3	EC	G
		Moycraig Hamilton	7	P	G
		Toberdoney	7,12	SP	G
20	Blaris	Broughmore	67	EC	
				M	
		Lisburn, Chapel Hill	68	RC	
					G
		Dublin Road		New EC	
		Linenhall Street		M	
		Market Place		M	
		Market Square		P	
				EC	
		Market Street		M	
		Railway Street		Q	G
21	Camlin	Ballydonagh	55,59		G
		Crumlin, Main Street	59	P	
				U	G
		Mill Road		Temporary M	

NGA No.	CIVIL PARISH	TOWNLAND OR TOWN, STREET	OS No.	CHURCH	GRAVE-YARD
22	Carncastle	Ballygalley	35	EC	G
		Corkermain	35	U	G
				P	
23	Carnmoney	Ballycraigy	51	I	
		Carnmoney	56,57	EC	G
		Village of Carnmoney	56,57	P	
		Village of Whiteabbey	52	P	
		White House	57	EC	
24	Carrickfergus or St. Nicholas	Carrickfergus, Castle Street	52	P	
		Irish Quarter West		M	
		Joymount Bank		P	
				REM	
		Market Place		EC	G
		Minorca Street		RC	G
		North Street		P	
		West Street		M	
		North East Division	46,47 52,53	RP	
					New G
		West Division	46,51 52	RC	
				EZ	
25	Connor	Carnaghts	37,38	P	G
		Connor	38,44	EC	G
		Village of Connor	38	P	
		Kells	38,44		G
		Village of Kells	38	M	
26	Craigs	Craigs	26,27 31,32	EC	G
		Cullybackey	32	P	
				COV	G
				Site of RC	

NGA No.	CIVIL PARISH	TOWNLAND OR TOWN, STREET	OS No.	CHURCH	GRAVE-YARD
26	Craigs	Dreen	32	I	G
27	Cranfield	Cranfield	49		G
28	Culfeightrin	Ballynaglogh	5,9	EC	G
		Barnish	5,9	RC	G
		Coolranny	10	RC	
		Cross	5		G
		Cushendun	15	EC	
		Drumadoon	9		G
		Drumnakeel	9		G
29	Derryaghy	Ballymacward Upper	59,60, 63,64	RC	
		Derryaghy	64	EC	G
		Islandkelly	59,63	EC	
		Lagmore	64	RC	
30	Derrykeighan	Carncoggy	12	P	
		Carncullagh Lower	12	P	G
		Town of Dervock, Coleraine Road	12	EC	
		Glebe	12		G
		Knockanboy	12	RC	
		Knockavallan	12	P	
31	Donegore	Donegore	50	EC	G
		Dunamuggy	44,45 50,51	SP	G
		Village of Parkgate	50,51	P	
32	Drumbeg	Dunmurry	64	P U	G
33	Drummaul	Ballygrooby	43,49	RC	G
		Craigmore	43,49	I	G
		Drummaul	43		G
		Feehogue	43	P	G
		Randalstown	43	1st. P	G
		Randalstown, Main Street	43	P EC	G

NGA No.	CIVIL PARISH	TOWNLAND OR TOWN, STREET	OS No.	CHURCH	GRAVE-YARD
33	Drummaul	Randalstown, Market Street	43	M	
34	Dunaghy	Cargan	24		G
		Carn-beg	27	P	
		Carrowcowan	24,28	RC	G
		Cloghaldanagh	27	EC	
		Glebe	27		G
35	Duneane	Ballylenully	42,43		G
				P	G
		Ballymatoskerty	42	RC	G
		Cargin	48	RC	
		Lismacloskey	42,48	EC	G
36	Dunluce	Town of Bushmills	3,7	RC	
		Dunluce	2,6		G
		Glebe	7	EC	G
		Walk Mill	7	P	
					G
37	Finvoy	Ballymacaldrack	22,23		G
		Dunloy	22,23	P	
				RC	
		Knockan	22		G
				EC	G
		Mullans	22	P	G
		Vow	21,22		G
38	Glenavy	Ballymacricket	59,63	RC	G
		Ballyvanen	58,62	MO	
		Deer Park	62	EC	
		Glenavy	59	EC	G
		Village of Glenavy	59	M	
39	Glenwhirry	Glenwhirry	39	P	
					G
40	Glynn	Glynn	40	EC	G
41	Grange of Ballyscullion	Grange Park	42	EC	
		Killylaes	36,42		G
		Mill Quarter	36,42	Q	

6

NGA No.	CIVIL PARISH	TOWNLAND OR TOWN, STREET	OS No.	CHURCH	GRAVE-YARD
41	Grange of Ballyscullion	Taylorstown	42,43	P	
					G
				BAP	
42	Grange of Doagh	Ballyclare	45,51	RC	
		Ballyclare, Back Street	45	RP	
		Doagh Road		BL	
				P	
		Main Street		U	
		Doagh	45,51		G
		Village of Doagh	51	M	
43	Grange of Drumtullagh	Carrowreagh	8	EC	
		Kilmoyle	8		G
44	Grange of Dundermot	Drumbare	23	P	G
45	Grange of Inispollen	Ardicoan	15	RC	G
46	Grange of Killyglen				
47	Grange of Layd				
48	Grange of Muckamore	Muckamore	50		G
				EC	G
		Shaneoguestown	50,55	P	
49	Grange of Nilteen				
50	Grange of Shilvodan	Eskylane	44	P	
		Tavnaghmore	43,44	RC	
51	Inver	Town of Larne, Point Street	40	1st. P	
52	Island Magee	Ballyharry	41	EC	
		Ballykeel	47		G
		Ballymoney	41	M	
		Ballyprior More	41		G
		Kilcoan More	41	P	
		Mullaghboy	41	P	
53	Kilbride	Kilbride	45,51	P	G
54	Killaghan	Drumadoon	23	EC	
55	Killead	Ballyquillin	34,55	RC	G
		Balmymather Lower	55,56	P	

COUNTY ANTRIM

NGA No.	CIVIL PARISH	TOWNLAND OR TOWN, STREET	OS No.	CHURCH	GRAVE-YARD
55	Killead	Gartee	58	EC	G
		Grange of Carmavy	55		G
		Seacash	54,55	EC	G
		Tully	55	P	G
56	Kilraghts	Carnageeragh	18	P	G
		Kilraghts	17,18	COV	G
				EC	G
		Magheraboy Lower	12,13 17,18	SP	G
57	Kilroot	Kilroot	53		G
58	Kilwaughter				
59	Kirkinriola	Ballymena, Ballymoney Road	32	P in Progress	
		Castle Street		M	
		Church Street			G
		High Street		P	
				U	
		Hill Street		BAP	
		Meeting House Lane		P	
		Wellington Street		P	
		Kirkinriola	32		G
		Townparks	32,37	RC	
				EC	
60	Lambeg	Lambeg North	64	EC	G
61	Larne	Larne, Church Road	40	EC	G
		Mill Street		U	
		Newton Street		COV	
		Pound Road		P	
				M	
				P	
		Townparks	40		G
				RC	
62	Layd	Cushendall	20	RC	

COUNTY ANTRIM

NGA No.	CIVIL PARISH	TOWNLAND OR TOWN, STREET	OS No.	CHURCH	GRAVE-YARD
62	Layd	Town of Cushendall, Mill Street	20	EC	
		Kilmore	19,20		G
		Moneyvart	15,20		G
		Mullarts	15	P	G
63	Loughguile	Ballyweeny	14	P	G
		Castlequarter	18	EC	
		Lavin Lower	18		G
		Magherahoney	13	RC	
		Tully North	18	RC	G
64	Magheragall	Ballycarrickmaddy	63	P	G
		Knocknadona	62	M	
		Magheragall	63,67	EC	G
65	Magheramesk	Ballynalargy	67	Q	
		Trummery	67		G
66	Newton Cromlin	Skerry East	24	P	
				EC	G
67	Portglenone	Garvaghy	31	P	G
				P	G
				EC	G
		Town of Portglenone	31	EZ	
				P	
		Slievenagh	31,36		G
				RC	G
68	Racavan	Ballynacaird	33,34	P	G
		Broughshane, Church Lane	32,33	EC	G
		Main Street		P	G
		Racavan	33,38		G
69	Raloo	Altilevelly	40,46	P	
		Ballygowan	40,46	RC	G
		Ballywillin	41,46	EC	G
		Tureagh	40,46	Meeting house	G
70	Ramoan	Ballycastle, Anne Street	8	EC	
		Castle Street		P	

9

NGA No.	CIVIL PARISH	TOWNLAND OR TOWN, STREET	OS No.	CHURCH	GRAVE-YARD
70	Ramoan	Ballycastle, Clare Street	8	M	
		Fair Hill Street		RC	
		Corvally	8,9, 14	RC	
		Glebe	8	EC	
					G
		Gortconny	4,8		G
		Moyagret Upper	8	P	
71	Rasharkin	Dromore	27	2nd. P	G
				1st. P	G
		Glebe	26	EC	G
		Moneyleck	26	P	G
				RC	G
72	Rashee	Rashee	45		G
73	Rathlin Island	Church Quarter	1	EC	G
				RC	
74	Shankill	Ballymurphy	60	EC	
				M	
		Village of Ballysillan	56,60	EC	
				P	
		Englishtown	60,64	RC	G
		Village of Green Castle	56,57	RC	G
		Village of Legoniel	56,60	M	
		Malone Lower	60,61 64,65	P	G
					Quaker G
		Malone Upper	64,65	EC	
		Tom of the Tae-End	64	EC	
75	Skerry	Aghafatten	28,29	RC	
		Lisnacrogher	27	P	
		Magheramully	28,33		G
76	Templecorran	Ballycarry North-West	47	P	
		Ballycarry South-West	47	P	

COUNTY ANTRIM

NGA No.	CIVIL PARISH	TOWNLAND OR TOWN, STREET	OS No.	CHURCH	GRAVE-YARD
76	Templecorran	Forthill	47	EC	G
77	Templepatrick	Ballybarnish	51,56	P	
		Craigarogan	51,56		Old G
		Grange of Molusk	56	M	G
		Grange of Umgall	56		G
		Kilgreel	51,56	P	
		Templepatrick	50,51		G
				EC	G
		Village of Templepatrick	50,51	P	
78	Tickmacrevan	Cloney	29	REM	G
		Deer Park Farms	29,34,35	RC	G
		Glebe	29		G
		Glenarm, Altmore Street	29	P	
		Vennel Street		M	
		Harphill	25,29	RC	
79	Tullyrusk	Dundrod	59,60	P	
		Tullyrusk	59		G

11

NGA No.	CIVIL PARISH	TOWNLAND OR TOWN, STREET	OS No.	CHURCH	GRAVE- YARD
1	Armagh	Armagh, Abbey Street	12	M	
				M	
				1st P	
		Cathedral Close		EC Cathedral	G
		Chapel Lane		RC	
		English Street Lower		2nd P	G
		Gosford Place		3rd P	
		The Mall		St.Marks EC	G
		Corporation	12		G
				RC Cathedral unfinished	
2	Ballymore	Village of Acton	18	M	
		Auglish	14,18		G
		Ballymore	13,14	EC	G
		Brannock	18		G
				RC	G
		Clare	13,17	P	
				SP	
		Derryallen	13,14	P	
		Federnagh	18	EC	G
		Lisnagree	18,22	P	G
		Mavemacullen	17	EC	
		Mullaghglass	14,18	RC	
		Tanderagee, Market Street	14	M	
				M	
				RC	
		Tannyoky	17,18	P	G
		Terryhoogan	14		G
		Tullynacross	18	P	G
3	Ballymyre	Ballintemple	20,21, 24,25	EC	G
		Knockavannon	21,25	RC	
4	Clonfeacle	Town of Blackwatertown	8	M	

NGA No.	CIVIL PARISH	TOWNLAND OR TOWN, STREET	OS No.	CHURCH	GRAVE- YARD
4	Clonfeacle	Tullyroan	4,8	M	
				M	
5	Creggan	Creggan Bane Glebe	30,31	EC	G
		Crossmaglen, Dundalk Street	30	M	
		Cullyhanna Big	27	RC	
		Freeduff	27,28	P	G
		Glassdrumman	31	RC	
		Monog	30	RC	G
		Moybane	30	Old RC	
6	Derrynoose	Listarkelt	19		G
		Maghery Kilcrany	11,12, 15,16		G
		Madden	15	RC	G
				EC	G
		Mowillin	15,16	P	G
7	Drumcree	Ballyworkan	9,10, 13	M	
		Derryall	5	M	
		Derryanvil	5	M	
		Drumcree	5,9	EC	G
		Drumnakelly	9,13	M	
				M	
		Portadown, Church Street	9	EC	
		Mary Street		M	
		Montague Street		M	
		Obins Street		M	
		Thomas Street		M	
		West Street		M	
		William Street		RC	
		Richmount or Aghavellan	9	M	
		Selshion	9	RC	G
		Timakeel	5,9	M	
8	Eglish	Cavanballaghy	11	P	G
		Drumsallan Upper	11	EC	G

13

NGA No.	CIVIL PARISH	TOWNLAND OR TOWN, STREET	OS No.	CHURCH	GRAVE- YARD
8	Eglish	Edenderry	7,8	EC	
		Eglish	7		G
		Tullysaran	7,8, 11,12	RC	G
9	Forkill	Village of Forkill	28,31	M	
		Shanroe	28,31	RC	G
		Shean	28,31	EC	G
10	Grange	Annacramph	8,12	RC	
		Salters Grange	8,12	EC	G
11	Jonesborough	Foughill Etra	29,32	P	
				EC in progress	G
		Village of Jonesborough	32	RC	
12	Keady	Aughnagurgan	20,24	P	G
		Crossnamoyle	19	RC	G
		Granemore	20	RC	G
		Keady, Chapel Street	20	RC	G
		Church Street		EC	G
		Main Street		M	
		Mill Street		P	G
		Tassagh	16,20		G
				P	G
13	Kilclooney	Ballylane	17,21	COV	
					G
		Cavangrow	16,17	P	G
		Clady More	20,21	P	
				RC	G
		Glassdrummond	17	EC	G
		Kilbracks	17		G
14	Kildarton	Drumennis	13	P	
		Tirnascobe	12	EC	G
15	Killevy	Ballintemple	28,29		G
		Village of Bessbrook	22,26	Q	
		Village of Camlough	26	EC	G

COUNTY ARMAGH

NGA No.	CIVIL PARISH	TOWNLAND OR TOWN, STREET	OS No.	CHURCH	GRAVE-YARD
15	Killevy	Village of Camlough	26	RC	G
		Cloghinny	22	EC	G
		Drumbanagher	22	EC	
		Drumintee	28,29, 32	RC	G
		Ellisholding	29	RC	
		Killeen	29	RC	G
		Kilmonaghan	22	P	G
		Knockduff	22	P	G
		Latt	22,26		G
		Lislea	25,28	RC	G
		Lissummon	22		G
				RC	G
		Maghernahely	26	P	
		Meigh	29	RC	
				EC	G
		Mullaghglass	22,26	EC	
16	Killyman	Clonmore	4	RC	G
17	Kilmore	Aghory	13	P	G
		Ballintaggart	9	P	G
				M	
		Drumnahunshin	9	RC	
		Kilmore	9	EC	G
		Money	9		G
		Mulladry	9,13	EC	G
		Mullavilly	13	EC	G
		Rich Hill, Broad Street	13	EC	
				I	
		Irish Street		P	G
				Q	
		Mill Street		M	
		Rockmacreeny	13	M	
		Tamnaghvelton	13	RC	
18	Lisnadill	Aghavilly	16	EC	G

15

NGA No.	CIVIL PARISH	TOWNLAND OR TOWN, STREET	OS No.	CHURCH	GRAVE-YARD
18	Lisnadill	Armaghbrague	20,24	EC	G
		Ballymacanab	16	RC	G
		Lisnadill	16	EC	G
19	Loughgall	Annaghmore	4,5	EC	G
		Ballymagerney	8	M	
		Town of Charlemont	4	M	
		Clonmain	4,8	M	
		Cloven Eden	8	P	G
		Corr and Dunvally	4,8		G
				EC	G
		Eagralougher	8	RC	
		Keenaghan	4,8	RC	
		Kinnegoe	8	M	
		Levalleglish	8	EC	
		Village of Loughgall	8		G
20	Loughgilly	Ballenan	17,18, 22	P	G
		Village of Belleek	25	RC	
		Carrickananny	25	RC	
		Carrickgallogly	25	EC	G
		Cornagrally	17,21	EC	G
		Lisadian	21	P	
		Mountnorris	17,21	P	G
		Tullyallen	17,21	P	G
		Tullyherron	21	RC	G
21	Magheralin				
22	Montiaghs	Derryadd	2,3, 5,6	EC	G
		Derryinver	2	M	
		Derrytagh North	2,5	P	
		Derrytrasna	2,5	RC	G
23	Mullaghbrack	Drumlack	17	RC	G
		Drumman	13	M	
		Markethill, Keady Street	17	M	
				P	G

NGA No.	CIVIL PARISH	TOWNLAND OR TOWN, STREET	OS No.	CHURCH	GRAVE-YARD
23	Mullaghbrack	Markethill, Main Street	17	EC	
		Water Lane		P	G
		Mullaghbrack	13,17	EC	G
24	Newry	Grange Lower	9	EC	
		Lisdrumgullion	26	RC	
		Newry, Catherine Street	26	Convent RC	
25	Newtownhamilton	Atlnamackan	24,27	P	
		Cortamlat	24	P	G
		Tullyvallan	20,24 25,27	RC	G
				P	
				SP	
				EC	G
26	Seagoe	Aghacommon	6	RC	G
		Ballygargan	10	EC	G
		Ballynacor	6	M	
		Lisnamintry	10	M	
		Lisnisky	6,10	M	
		Lylo	·10	RC	G
		Moyraverty	6,10		Quaker G
		Township of Portadown	9,10	M	
		Portadown, Bridge Street	9,10	P	
				BAP	
		Seagoe Lower	5,6, 9,10		G
		Seagoe Upper	9,10	EC	
27	Shankill	Township of Lurgan	6		G
		Town of Lurgan	6		G
		Lurgan, Church Place	6	EC	
		High Street		M	
				1st P	G
				Q	G
		Hill Street		2nd P	
		North Street		RC	

NGA No.	CIVIL PARISH	TOWNLAND OR TOWN, STREET	OS No.	CHURCH	GRAVE-YARD
27	Shankill	Lurgan, Queen Street	6	M	
		Monbrief	6,10		G
28	Tartaraghan	Ballynarry	5	P	G
		Breagh	5	EC	G
		Cloncore	5	M	
		Derrinraw	2,5	M	
		Derryaugh	2	EC	G
		Derrylee	1,4	M	
		Eglish	5	RC	G
		Maghery	1,2	RC	G
29	Tynan	Cavandoogan	15	RC	G
		Drumhillery	15,19	P	
		Village of Killylea	11	EC M	G
		Lisloony	11,15	P	
		Middletown	15	P	
		Shantally	15	EC	G
		Tynan	11,15	RC	G
		Village of Tynan	11	EC	G

NGA No.	CIVIL PARISH	TOWNLAND OR TOWN, STREET	OS No.	CHURCH	GRAVE-YARD
50 Down	Knockbreda	Ballynafoy Road	50,55, 59,60 61,62	P	
		Ballynafoy Village	55,59	M	
		Chapel Lane	31,38	RC	
		Lagan Bridge Road	38	P	
		Newtownards Road	31,32 39	M	
				M	G
				EC	
74 Antrim	Shankill	Academy Street	23,29 30	BAP	
		Agnes Street	21,28	M	
		Albert Place	43	Magdalene EC	
		Albert Street	35,36	P	
		Alexander Street West	28,29	Site of new RC	
		Alfred Street	37	P	
		Berry Street	29	P	
		Blackstaff Lane	42,43		G
		Chapel Lane	29	St.Marys RC	
		Clarence Street	36	St.Malachi's RC	
		Clarendon Place	37	P	
		College Square North	36	Christ-church EC	
		College Street South	36	RP	
		Corporation Street	23,30	Sinclair Seamens P	
		Crumlin Road	14,21 22	Convent RC	
		Derby Street	28	RC in Progress	

NGA No.	CIVIL PARISH	TOWNLAND OR TOWN, STREET	OS No.	CHURCH	GRAVE-YARD
74 Antrim	Shankill	Donegall Place	29,36	M	
		Donegall Square East	36,37	M	
		Donegall Street	22,29, 30	St.Annes EC	
				I	
				St. Patricks RC	
				P	
		Eglinton Street	22	P	
		Falls Road	28,29	M	
		Fisherwick Place	36	P	
		Frederick Street	22	M	
				Q	
		Friar's Bush, Road	49,54		G
		Great George's Street	22,23	P	
		Great Victoria Street	36,43	New P	
		Henry Place	22		G
		High Street	30	St. Georges EC	
		Linenhall Street	36	P	
				RP	
		Melbourne Street	29	M	
		Milford Street	28,29, 35	Site of New RC	
		Mill Lane	36	M	
		Queen Street	29,36	RC	
		Rosemary Street	29	P	
				1st.U	
				2nd.U	
		St. John's Street	37	St. John's EC	

NGA No.	CIVIL PARISH	TOWNLAND OR TOWN, STREET	OS No.	CHURCH	GRAVE-YARD
74 Antrim	Shankill	Shankill Road	13,20 21	St. Matthews EC	
					Shankill G
		Townsend Street	29	P	
		Unity Street	22	Trinity EC	
		University Road	43,49	Elm Wood P in Progress	
		Wellington Place	36	Evangel- ical Union Church	
		Wesley Place	43	M	
		York Road	16	St.Pauls EC	
		York Street	16,23	Salem M	
				SP	
				P	
		York Street	22,29	U	

NGA No.	CIVIL PARISH	TOWNLAND OR TOWN, STREET	OS No.	CHURCH	GRAVE-YARD
1	Agha	Agha	12,16		G
		Newtown	12,16	RC	G
2	Aghade	Aghade	13	EC	G
3	Ardoyne	Ardattin	13,14	RC	
4	Ardristan	Ardristan	13		G
5	Ballinacarrig	Ballinacarrig	7		G
		Quinagh	7		G
		Staplestown	7	EC	
6	Ballon	Village of Ballon	13	RC	G
7	Ballycrogue				
8	Ballyellin	Ballyellin and Tomdarragh	19,22		G
9	Baltinglass				
10	Barragh	Barragh	17		G
		Crowsgrove	18	RC	G
		Kilbrannish South	20,23		G
		Kildavin	18,21		G
		Village of Kildavin	18,21	EC	G
11	Carlow	Carlow, Athy Street	7	P	G
		Castle Hill			G
		Chapel Lane		Present-ation Convent	
				Convent Chapel	
				RC	
				College Chapel	
		Charlotte Street		M	
		Church Street		EC	G
		Dublin Road		Convent Chapel	
				Convent	
		Grave Lane			G
12	Clonmelsh	Clonmelsh	12	EC	G
		Garryhundon	12		G

NGA No.	CIVIL PARISH	TOWNLAND OR TOWN, STREET	OS No.	CHURCH	GRAVE-YARD
13	Clonmore	Glebe	9	EC	G
		Oldtown	9	RC	G
14	Clonygoose	Borris	22	EC	
		Town of Borris	22	RC	
		Clonygoose	22		G
15	Cloydagh	Ballinabranagh	6,12	RC	G
		Cloghna	7,12		G
		Clogrenan	6,7		G
		Killeeshal	7	EC	
16	Crecrin	Crecrin	4		G
17	Dunleckny	Bagenalstown, Chapel Street	16	RC	
		Old Post Office Street		M	
		Regent Street		Convent Chapel	
		Curraghacruit	16		G
		Dunleckny	16		G
18	Fennagh	Ballybrommell	12,13,16		G
		Ballykealey	13		G
		Castlemore	8,13		G
		Drumfea	19,20	RC	G
		Fennagh	16,17	EC	G
		Kilconner	17	Q	
		Tullowbeg	8,13		G
19	Gilbertstown	Gilbertstown	13		G
		Rathoe	8,13	RC	
20	Grangeford	Grangeford Old	8		G
		Slaneyquarter	8	RC	G
21	Hacketstown	Hacketstown, Main Street	4	RC	
		Penny Hill		EC	G
				M	
22	Haroldstown	Haroldstown	4,9		G
23	Kellistown	Ballyveal	13		G
		Kellistown East	8,13	EC	G

NGA No.	CIVIL PARISH	TOWNLAND OR TOWN, STREET	OS No.	CHURCH	GRAVE- YARD
24	Killerrig	Busherstown	7,8		G
		Killerig	3,8		G
25	Killinane	Closutton	16		G
26	Kiltegan	Tinnaclash	4		G
27	Kiltennell	Ballinvally and Kiltennell	22		G
		Killemond	22,23	EC	G
		Rathanna	23	RC	G
28	Kineagh	Ballycook	3		G
				EC	
29	Lorum	Ballinkillin	19	RC	G
		Lorum	19	EC	G
					G
30	Moyacomb	Clonegall	18	EC	G
		Town of Clonegall	18	RC	G
				M	
31	Myshall	Ballaghmore	17		G
		Village of Myshall	17	EC	G
				RC	G
					G
32	Nurney	Nurney, Carlow Street	12	EC	G
33	Oldleighlin	Oldleighlin	11	EC	G
34	Painestown	Newgarden	2		G
35	Rahill	Rahill	1,3,4		G
36	Rathmore				
37	Rathvilly	Knocklishenbeg	4		G
		Rathvilly	3,4	EC	G
		Town of Rathvilly	4	RC	G
		Tiknock	4	RC	
		Tobinstown	4,9		G
		Waterstown	4		G
38	St. Mullin's	Bahana	24,26	RC	
		Ballymurphy	22	RC	G
		Drummin	26	RC	
		St. Mullin's	26	EC	G

NGA No.	CIVIL PARISH	TOWNLAND OR TOWN, STREET	OS No.	CHURCH	GRAVE-YARD
38	St Mullins	Tinnahinch	24		G
39	Sliguff	Seskinnamadra	19,20		G
		Sliguff	19		G
40	Straboe				
41	Templepeter	Templepeter	12,13		G
42	Tullowcreen	Craanlusky	6,11	EC	
		Tomard Lower	11,12		G
43	Tullowmagimma	Linkardstown	12		G
		Tinriland	7,12	RC	G
44	Tullowphelim	Tullow, Church Street	8	EC	G
		Mullaun Hill			G
		New Chapel		RC	
				Monastery Chapel	
				St Bridgets Convent Chapel	
		Old Chapel Lane		M	
45	Ullard				
46	Urglin	Bennekerry	7	RC	G
		Urglin or Rutland	7	EC	G
47	Wells	Ballyknockan	11,12, 16	RC	
				EC	G
		Wells	15,16		G

COUNTY CAVAN

NGA No.	CIVIL PARISH	TOWNLAND OR TOWN, STREET	OS No.	CHURCH	GRAVE-YARD
1	Annagelliff	Annagelliff	20,25		G
		Stragelliff	20,21	RC	
2	Annagh	Annagh	15		G
		Belturbet, Bridge Street	11,15	M	
		Chapel Lane		M	
				RC	
		Church Street		EC	
		Deanery Street		P	
		Clonosey	11,15		G
		Cloverhill Demesne	15	Church in Progress	
		Castlesaunderson	11	EC	
		Drumalee	11,15	RC	
		Drumeena	16	EC	G
		Glasdrumman	16	RC	
		Mullalougher	16	M	
3	Bailieborough	Bailieborough, Cootehill Road	34	M	
		Henry Street		RC	
		Drumbannan	28,34	EC	G
		Killan	28		G
		Lisgar	25	P	G
		Urcher	34	P	G
4	Ballintemple	Aghaloory	31,37	RC	
		Ballintemple	31	EC	G
		Brusky	31	RC	
		Pottahee	31	RC	G
5	Ballymachugh	Lavagh	37,38	EC	G
		Omard	37,38	RC	
6	Castlerahan	Ballyjamesduff, Dublin Street	38	M	
		Market Street		M	
		Oldcastle Street		RC	
		Castlerahan	38	EC	G
		Cormeen	38,39	RC	

COUNTY CAVAN

NGA No.	CIVIL PARISH	TOWNLAND OR TOWN, STREET	OS No.	CHURCH	GRAVE-YARD
6	Castlerahan	Crosserule Deer Park	38,39	P	
7	Castleterra	Castleterra	21	RC	G
		Town Parks	15,16 20,21	EC	G
				RC	
8	Crosserlough	Carrickacroy	32,38	EC	G
		Crosserlough	32,38	RC	G
		Cullow	32	RC	G
		Drumkilly	31	RC	
		Kill	31,37		G
9	Denn	Carrickaboy Glebe	25,26, 31,32		G
		Carrickatober	32	RC	
		Denn Glebe	26	EC	G
		Drumnavaddy	25,31	RC	
10	Drumgoon	Bellamont	17	EC	
		Cootehill, Bridge Street	17	P	
				M	
		Cavan Old Road		M	
		Chapel Lane		RC	
		Church Street			G
		Meeting House Row		SP	
		Corcreeghagh	17	RC	
		Dernakesh	22	EC	
		Drumaveil North	17	Q	
		Drumgoon	22		G
		Killatee	22,23	RC	
		Magheranure	17	MO	
11	Drumlane	Belturbet, Kilconny Street	14,15	RC	G
		Drumlane	14,15		G
		Killynaher	14	EC	G
		Village of Milltown	14	RC	
		Quivvy	11	EC	
12	Drumluman	Bracklagh	41	EC	G
		Carrick	41	RC	G

NGA No.	CIVIL PARISH	TOWNLAND OR TOWN, STREET	OS No.	CHURCH	GRAVE-YARD
12	Drumluman	Drumhawnagh	30,31 37	RC	G
		Mullaghhoran	37	RC	G
13	Drumreilly				
14	Drung	Doocassan	16,21	EC	
		Drumauna	16,21	RC	
		Drung	21		G
		Lisboduff	16	RC	
		Magherintemple	16		G
15	Enniskeen	Corlea	29	RC	
		Enniskeen	35		G
		Kingscourt, Chapel Hill	35	RC	G
		Church Street		M	
				EC	G
		Laragh	35	RC	
16	Kilbride	Gallonreagh	38		G
		Mountnugent	38	RC	G
				EC	G
17	Kildallan	Coolnashinny or Croaghan	19	P	G
		Kildallan	14	EC	G
					G
		Killygreagh	14	RC	
18	Kildrumsherdan	Corballyquill	17	EC	
		Corbeagh	17		G
		Drumhurt	17,22		G
				EC	G
				RC	G
		Drummury	17	RC	
		Tonaghbane	17	EC	G
		Tullyvin	17		G
19	Killashandra	Aghnacor	24	EC	G
		Corlisbrattan	24	M	
		Corranea	24	RC	
		Drumalt	24,30	RC	

COUNTY CAVAN

NGA No.	CIVIL PARISH	TOWNLAND OR TOWN, STREET	OS No.	CHURCH	GRAVE-YARD
19	Killashandra	Drumkilroosk	24	P	
		Drumroosk	19		G
		Killashandra, Church Street	19		G
		Main Street		EC	
		Yewer Lane		M	
		Portaliff	19	RC	
		Ticosker	24,30	EC	
20	KIllinagh	Corradeverrid	5	EC	
		Corraquigley	3	RC	
		Killycarney	1,2	RC	
		Termon	2	EC	G
		Thornhill or Mullan Dreenagh	1	EC	G
		Tuam	2	M	
21	Killinkere	Beagh Glebe	33	EC	
		Carrickeeshil	33	EC	G
		Corratinner	33	RC	
		Gallon	33		G
		Gola	27,33	P	
		Termon	33	RC	
22	Kilmore	Bellanagh	25	RC	G
		Drumcor	20,25	RC	
		Kilmore Upper	20,25	EC	G
		Trinity Island	19,20	Trinity Abbey in ruins	G
23	Kinawley	Furnaceland	7	EC	G
				M	
				M	
		Swanlinbar, Main Street	7	RC	
24	Knockbride	Drumamuck Glebe	23,28	RC	
		Knockbride	23	RC	
				EC	
		Lisdonan	23,28	P	
		Roosky	23	P	

29

NGA No.	CIVIL PARISH	TOWNLAND OR TOWN, STREET	OS No.	CHURCH	GRAVE- YARD
24	Knockbride	Tonyduff	27	RC	G
25	Larah	Carrickallen	22,27	RC	
		Clifferna	26,27	RC	
		Killycrone	21,26	EC	
		Larah	21		G
		Monelty	21,26	RC	
26	Lavey	Killyconnan	26	RC	
		Knocknagillagh	26,32	RC	
		Lavey	26	EC	G
27	Loughan or Castlekeeran	Edenburt	43,44	EC	
28	Lurgan	Coppanagh Glebe	39	RC	
		Drumgora	33,39	P	
		Lurgan	39		G
		Pollintemple	43	RC	
		Virginia, Main Street	39	EC	
				RC	
29	Moybolgue	Relaghbeg	38,40		G
30	Mullagh	Cornakill	40	RC	
		Crossreagh	40	RC	
		Mullagh	41,44	EC	G
31	Munterconnaught	Knockatemple	39,43	RC	G
				EC	
32	Scrabby	Cloone	30,36	EC	G
		Scrabby	30,36	RC	G
33	Shercock	Killcrossbeg	28	RC	
		Lisdrumskea	23	RC	
		Ralaghan	28	P	G
		Shercock, Main Streeet	23	EC	G
34	Templeport	Arderry	9,13	RC	
		Gub or Galvalt Upper	6	RC	G
		Kildoag	9	RC	
		Kilnavert	13	RC	G
		Port	9,13	EC	G
					G

NGA No.	CIVIL PARISH	TOWNLAND OR TOWN, STREET	OS No.	CHURCH	GRAVE-YARD
35	Tomregan	Ballyconnell, Bawnboy Road	10	EC	G
		Main Street		M	
		Cullyleenan	10	RC	
36	Urney	Cavan, Bridge Street	20	M	
		Church Lane	20	Abbey Ruins	G
		Church Place		EC	G
		Farnham Street	20	RC	
				P	
		Wesleyan Street		M	
		Derryheen	20	EC	G
		Drumgola	20	RC	
		Keadew	20		G
		Urney	15		G

COUNTY CLARE

NGA No.	CIVIL PARISH	TOWNLAND OR TOWN, STREET	OS No.	CHURCH	GRAVE-YARD
1	Abbey	Abbey West	3		G
		Ballyvelaghan	3	EC	
		Dooneen	3	RC	
		Mortyclogh	3		G
2	Bunratty	Bunratty West	51,61,62		G
		Clonmoney West	51,61	RC	
3	Carran	Ballyconry	10	RC	
		Ballyline	9,10		G
		Coolnatullagh	6		G
		Glencolumbkille North	6,10		G
		Glencolumbkille South	10		G
		Keelhilla	6		G
		Poulacarran	9		G
		Termon	6,10		G
4	Clareabbey	Clareabbey	33,41		G
		Clarehill	41,42		G
		Clare, Ennis Road	41	RC	
		Main Street	41,42	EC	
		Killow	33,42		G
5	Clondagad	Gortygeeheen	49		G
		Knockalehid	50	EC	G
		Lanna	49,50	RC	
		Lisheen	50		G
		Toberaniddaun	49		G
6	Clonlea	Clonlea	43		G
		Gortnacorragh	43	EC	
		Village of Kilkishen	35,43	RC	
		Oatfield	42,52,53	RC	
7	Clonloghan	Clonloghan	51		G
8	Clonrush				
9	Clooney	Clooney	34	RC	
					G
		Clooney South	16,24		G

32

COUNTY CLARE

NGA No.	CIVIL PARISH	TOWNLAND OR TOWN, STREET	OS No.	CHURCH	GRAVE-YARD
9	Clooney	Killeinagh	15,23		G
		Knockaphreaghaun	34		G
		Mooghna	23		G
		Muckinish	34		G
		Teerleheen	24	RC (old) RC in Progress	
10	Doora	Castletown	34		G
		Kilbreckan	34		G
		Noughaval	34	RC	G
11	Drumcliff	Drumcliff	25,33		G
		Ennis, The Causeway	33	M	
		Church Street		EC	G
		Friary Lane		Franciscan Friary Chapel	
		Goal Street		RC	
		McNamara's Lane		Friary Chapel (Unfinished)	
		Lifford	33		G
		Mahonburgh	33,41	RC	
12	Drumcreehy	Muckinish West	2,3	RC	
13	Drumline	Drumline	51		G
14	Dysert	Kilcurrish	25,33		G
		Killeenan	25	RC	
		Mollaneen	25		G
15	Feakle	Caher (Power)	19,20		G
		Dereendooagh	12,13		G
		Fahy	19		G
		Feakle	20,28	RC EC	G

NGA No.	CIVIL PARISH	TOWNLAND OR TOWN, STREET	OS No.	CHURCH	GRAVE-YARD
15	Feakle	Flagmount	20	RC	
					G
		Gortavrulla	20		G
		Kilclaran	20	RC	
		Killanena	12,19	RC	G
		Knockalisheen	28		G
16	Feenagh	Feenagh (Wilson)	51,52		G
17	Gleninagh	Gleninagh North	2		G
		Murrooghkilly	1,2		G
18	Inagh	Carrowkeel West	24,32	RC	
					G
		Gortbofarna	24		Childrens G
		Muckinish	24		G
19	Inchicronan	Ballinruan	18,19	RC	
		Cappafeean	26		G
		Carrowkeel More	18,26		G
		Crusheen	18,26		G
		Village of Crusheen	18,26	RC	
		Inchicronan Island	26		G
		Kilvoydan South	26,34		G
20	Inishcaltra				
21	Kilballyowen	Cross	65,72	RC	
22	Kilchreest	Carrowkilla	50		G
		Mount	50	RC	
23	Kilconry	Rineanna North	51,60 61		G
24	Kilcorney	Kilcorney Glebe	9		G
25	Kilfarboy	Freaghcastle	22,30		G
		Kilcorcoran	31		G
		Kildeema South	30,31		G
		Kilfarboy	23		G
		Milltown Malbay, Chapel Street	30,31	RC	
		Mullagh Road	30	EC	G

NGA No.	CIVIL PARISH	TOWNLAND OR TOWN, STREET	OS No.	CHURCH	GRAVE-YARD
26	Kilfearagh	Baunmore	56		G
		Emlagh	56		G
		Farrihy	46		G
		Kilfearagh	56,66		G
		Kilkee, Albert Road	56	M	
		Chapel Street		RC	
		Church Road		EC	
		Kilnagalliagh	56		G
		Lisdeen	56	RC	
27	Kilfenora	Town of Kilfenora	16	RC	
		Kilfenora, Well Lane	9,16	EC	G
28	Kilfiddane	Carrowreagh East	49,59	RC	
		Coolmeen	22,23	RC	
		Moyfadda	69		G
29	Kilfinaghta	Ballymulcashel	43,52	RC	
		Sixmilebridge, Church Street	52	EC	G
		The Green		RC	
30	Kilfintinan	Ballinphunta	52,56		G
		Ballybroughan	52		G
		Ballymorris	62	RC	
		Town of Sixmilebridge	52	RC	
					G
31	Kilkeedy	Creggaunycahill	18	RC	
		Cross	11		G
		Garryncallaha	17		G
		Kiltackymore	6,7,10,11		G
		Kylecreen	11	RC	
		Shanballysallagh	18		G
		Templebannagh	11	EC	
32	Killadysert	Coney Island	50,59,60		G
		Killadysert	59,60	EC	
					G
		Village of Killadysert	59,60	RC	

NGA No.	CIVIL PARISH	TOWNLAND OR TOWN, STREET	OS No.	CHURCH	GRAVE-YARD
33	Killaloe	Carrownakilly	36,37		G
		Killaloe, Chapel Street	45	RC	
		John's Street		M	
		Royal Parade		EC	G
		Lackenbaun	45	RC	
34	Killard	Cloonmore	38,47		G
		Village of Doonbeg	46,47	RC	G
		Doonmore	46,47	EC	G
		Killard	46		G
		Tullaher	46,56, 57		G
35	Killaspuglonane	Caheraderry	15	RC	
		Killaspuglonane	15		G
36	Killeany	Ballyconnoe North	8,9	RC	
		Killeany	5,8, 9		G
37	Killeely	Knockroe	62	EC	
		Moneennagliggin South	52,62		G
		Stonepark	62	RC	
38	Killilagh	Ballyvoe	8	RC	
		Killilagh	8		G
		Oughtdarra	4		G
39	Killimer	Burrane Lower	68		G
		Carrowdotia North	67	RC	
40	Killinaboy	Bunnanagat South	17	RC	
		Coad	17		G
		Town of Corrofin, Church Street	17	RC	
				EC	G
		Killinaboy	17		G
		Kilvoydan	17		G
41	Killofin	Killofin	68	RC	
					G
42	Killokennedy	Kilbane	36,44	RC	
		Killokennedy	36,44		G
		Kilmore	44,53	RC	G

COUNTY CLARE

NGA No.	CIVIL PARISH	TOWNLAND OR TOWN, STREET	OS No.	CHURCH	GRAVE-YARD
43	Killonaghan	Craggagh	4		G
		Formoyle East	1,2, 5		G
		Formoyle West	1,2, 4,5	RC	
44	Killone	Lismullreeda	41		G
		Newhall	41		G
		Teermaclane	41	RC	
45	Killuran	Iragh	35,36	RC	
		Killuran	36		G
46	Kilmacduane	Creegh South	47	RC	
		Drumellihy (Westropp)	47		G
		Kilmacduane East	47,48, 58		G
		Kilmacduane West	47,48, 57,58	RC	
47	Kilmacrehy	Derreen	14		G
		Dough	15,23		G
		Laghcloon	15		G
		Liscannor	14,15, 22,23	RC	
48	Kilmaleery	Clenagh	51	RC	
		Kilmaleery	51		G
49	Kilmaley	Feighroe	32	RC	
		Gartaganniv	32,33	EC	
		Kilmaley	32,33, 40,41	RC	
					G
50	Kilmanaheen	Calluragh South	23		G
		Deerpark West	15,23	RC	
					G
		Ennistimon	16		G
		Town of Ennistimon, Chapel Road	15,23	RC	
		Town of Lehinch, Chapel Street	15,23	RC	
		Sroohil	15	EC	

COUNTY CLARE

NGA No.	CIVIL PARISH	TOWNLAND OR TOWN, STREET	OS No.	CHURCH	GRAVE- YARD
51	Kilmihil	Village of Kilmihill	48	RC	
					G
52	Kilmoon	Kilmoon West	4,8		G
53	Kilmurry	Drumdigus	58	RC	
		Killernan	31,39		G
		Kilmurry East	58	EC	G
		Village of Kilmurry	38		G
		Village of Mullagh	38		G
				RC	
54	Kilnamona	Ballynabinnia	25,33	RC	
		Kilnamona	33		G
55	Kilnasoolagh	Kilnasoolagh	42,51	EC	G
56	Kilnoe	Coolready	28,36	RC	
		Kilnoe	28,36		G
57	Kilraghtis	Ballymaconna	26		G
58	Kilrush	Kilcarroll	67		G
		Kilrush, Burton Street	67	M	
		Grace Street		EC	G
		Toler Street		RC	
		Knockerry West	57,58	RC	
		Leadmore West	67		G
		Molougha	67		G
		Scattery Island	67		G
59	Kilseily	Clonsheerea	53		G
		Hurdlestown	44	EC	G
		Kilseily	44		G
		Kyle	44		G
		O'Shea's Acres	44	RC	
60	Kilshanny	Carrowreagh	8,15	RC	
		Porsoon	15		G
61	Kiltenanlea	Cloonlara	53	EC	G
				RC	
		Doonass Demesne	53,54		G
		Garraun	63		G

NGA No.	CIVIL PARISH	TOWNLAND OR TOWN, STREET	OS No.	CHURCH	GRAVE-YARD
62	Kiltoraght	Toormore	16	RC	
63	Moyarta	Village of Carrigaholt	65	RC	
		Doonaha West	66	RC	
		Lisheencrony	65,66		G
		Moyarta West	65		G
64	Moynoe	Moynoe	21,29		G
65	Noughaval	Noughaval	9	RC	
		Noughaval Glebe	9		G
66	O'Briensbridge	Ardtaggle	53,54	RC	G
		Cloghera	53	RC	
		Faghybeg	44,45, 53		G
		Inishlosky Island	54		G
		Town of O'Briensbridge	44,54	EC	G
		Ross	45		G
		Trough	53		G
67	Ogonnelloe	Ballylaghnan	37	RC	G
		Carrowcore	29,37	RC	
		Islandcosgry	29,37		G
		Rahena Beg	29,37	EC	
68	Oughtmama	Kilweelran	2,3, 5,6		G
69	Quin	Dangan	34,35		G
		Quin	42	RC, Old Abbey	G
		Village of Quin	42	EC	G
70	Rath	Craggaunboy	16,24		G
		Liscullaun	17,25	RC	
		Rath	25		G
71	Rathborney	Croagh North	5	RC	G
72	Ruan	Ruan Commons	25	RC	
73	St. Munchins	Knockalisheen	53,63		G

NGA No.	CIVIL PARISH	TOWNLAND OR TOWN, STREET	OS No.	CHURCH	GRAVE-YARD
74	St. Patricks	Ballykeelaun	53,63	RC	
		Kilquane	63		G
		Parteen	63	EC	
75	Templemaley	Barefield or Gortlumman	26	RC	
		Killian	25,26		G
76	Tomfinlough	Finlough	42		G
		Town of Newmarket on Fergus, The Green	42,51	RC	
77	Tomgraney	Callahy	28		G
		Cappacannaun	20,28		G
		Capparoe	28		G
		Cloonusker	20,28	RC	
		Coologory	20,28		G
		Fossa Beg	28	RC	
		Village of Tomgraney	28	RC	
				EC	
78	Tulla	Cragroe	27,35	RC	
		Glendree	19,27		G
		Tulla	35	EC	G
		Tulla, Chapel Street	35	RC	
		Market House Lane and Fair Hill			G

NGA No.	CIVIL PARISH	TOWNLAND OR TOWN, STREET	OS No.	CHURCH	GRAVE-YARD
1M	Abbeymahon	Ardgehane	136	EC	
		Village of Lislevane	136	RC	
1W	Abbeystrowry	Abbeystrowry	141		G
		Town of Skibbereen, Bridgetown	141	EC M	
2M	Aghabulloge	Coolineagh	60,61	EC	G
		Dromatimore	61	RC	
		Killerrihert	60	RC	
		Roylane	49,60, 61	RC	
		Rusheen	60,71	EC	
1E	Aghacross	Aghacross	18,19		G
2E	Aghada	Village of Aghada Lower	88	EC	
		Village of Aghada Upper	88	RC	G
2W	Aghadown	Glebe	141	EC	G
		Lisheen Lower	140,149	RC	
3E	Aghern	Aghern East	36,45	EC	G
3M	Aghinagh	Ballyvongane	60	RC	
		Caum	71	RC EC	G
4M	Aglish	Aglish	72		G
		Farran	72,84	RC	
5M	Aglishdrinagh	Ballycoskery	8	RC	
4E	Ardagh	Ballyneague	56,67	EC	G
		Barnaviddane	55,56	RC	
3W	Ardfield	Dunnycove	144	EC	G
		Mountain Common	135,144	RC	
5E	Ardnageehy	Ardnageehy West	52,53		G
		Village of Glenville	43,52	EC RC	G
		Town of Watergrasshill	53	RC	
6M	Ardskeagh	Ardskeagh	3,8		G

NGA No.	CIVIL PARISH	TOWNLAND OR TOWN, STREET	OS No.	CHURCH	GRAVE-YARD
7M	Athnowen	Carrigane	73	EC	G
		Knockanemore	72,73, 84,85	RC	
8M	Ballinaboy	Ballinaboy	86,97, 98	EC	G
		Gogganshill	85,97	RC	
9M	Ballinadee	Village of Ballinadee	111	EC	G
				RC	
6E	Ballintemple	Churchtown	89	RC	
					G
10M	Ballyclogh	Ballyclogh	24	RC	
		Village of Ballyclogh, Main Street	24	EC	G
7E	Ballycurrany	Ballycurrany West	65		G
8E	Ballydeloher	Brooklodge Upper	64	EC	G
9E	Ballydeloughy	Ballydeloughy	19		G
		Castleterry	19	RC	
10E	Ballyfeard	Ballingarry West	112	RC	
		Ballinluig West	98,112		G
				EC	
11E	Ballyfoyle	Ballyfoyle	113		G
11M	Ballyhay	Ballyhay	2,3, 7,8		G
12E	Ballyhooly	Ballyhooly North	26,34		G
				EC	G
		Village of Ballyhooly, Main Street	34,35	RC	
12M	Ballymartle	Curra	98	RC	
		Mill-Land	98	EC	G
13M	Ballymodan	Bandon, Cavendish Quay	110	M	
		Gallows Hill	110	RC	
		South Main Street	110	Bally-modan EC	
		Wesley Quay	110	M	
		Clogheenavodig	110		G
		Cloghmacsimon, Bradys Lane	110	U	

NGA No.	CIVIL PARISH	TOWNLAND OR TOWN, STREET	OS No.	CHURCH	GRAVE-YARD
13M	Ballymodan	Knockanreagh	110		G
		Knockaveale	110		G
4W	Ballymoney	Ballynacarriga	108	RC	
		Derrigra	109	M	G
		Knockaneady	108,109	EC	G
13E	Ballynoe	Ballinlegane	45,46	RC	
		Ballynoe	46		G
14E	Ballyoughtera	Castlemartyr	77		G
		Farrantrenchard	77	RC	
15E	Ballyspillane				
5W	Ballyvourney	Flats	58	RC	
		Glebe	58	EC	G
17E	Barnahely	Barnahely	87		G
18E	Bohillane	Garrananassig	77		G
14M	Bregoge				
19E	Bridgetown	Bridgetown Lower	26,34	EC	
20E	Brigown	Ballygiblin	20	RC	
		Mitchelstown, Cork Street Upper	19	RC	
		Georges Street		EC	G
		Kingston Square		EC	G
		Mulberry Lane			G
		Newmarket Square		RC	G
15M	Brinny	Brinny	96	EC	G
21E	Britway	Britway	45	EC (Ruins)	G
16M	Buttevant	Town of Buttevant, Main Street	16,17	RC	
		Castle-Land	17	EC	G
		Templemary	16	RC	
					G
6W	Caheragh	Cagheragh	119,132		G
		Coarliss	132	EC	
		Cooranuller	132,141		G

NGA No.	CIVIL PARISH	TOWNLAND OR TOWN, STREET	OS No.	CHURCH	GRAVE-YARD
6W	Caheragh	Dromore	119	RC	
		Killeenleagh	132	RC	
17M	Caherduggan	Clogheen	25		G
22E	Caherlag	Kilcoolishal	75		G
		Village of New Glanmire	75	RC	
18M	Cannaway	Bawnatemple	71	EC RC	G
23E	Carrigaline	Ballygarvan	86	RC	
		Carrigaline Middle	87	EC	G
		Village of Douglas	74,86	EC RC	G
		Moneygurney	86,87		G
		Shanbally	87	RC	
24E	Carrigdownane	Carrigdownane Lower	18,19 26,27		
25E	Carrigleamleary	Carrig Demesne	33	EC	G
19M	Carrigrohane	Ballincollig Village, Chapel Street	73	RC	
		Carrigrohane	73,74	EC	G
20M	Carrigrohanebeg	Carrigrohanebeg	73		G
26E	Carrigtohill	Village of Carrigtohill	75,76	RC EC	G
		Kilcurfin Glebe	75		G
7W	Castlehaven	Castlehaven	151		G
		Castletownsend	142,151	EC	G
		Drishane	142,151	RC	
27E	Castlelyons	Village of Bridebridge	45	RC	
		Kill-Saint-Anne-South	44,45	EC	
21M	Castlemagner	Castlemagner	23,24	EC	G
		Lisduggan South	23	RC	
28E	Castletownroche	Castletownroche	26	RC	
		Castletownroche, Chapel Road	26	Ground for RC	

NGA No.	CIVIL PARISH	TOWNLAND OR TOWN, STREET	OS No.	CHURCH	GRAVE-YARD
28E	Castletownroche	Castletownroche, Church Lane	26	EC	G
		Castletownroche, Old Doneraile Road		RC	
8W	Castleventry	Castleventry	134		G
		Coolcraheen	134	EC	
22M	Churchtown	Churchtown	7,16	EC	G
		Village of Churchtown, Buttevant Road	7,16	RC	
		Georges Street			G
9W	Clear Island	Glen Middle	153	EC	
		Lissamona	153	RC	
29E	Clenor	Annakisha North	25	RC	
		Clenor North	25	EC	G
23M	Clondrohid	Cadroma	69,70	RC	
		Garranenagapp	59,70	RC	
30E	Clondulane	Clondulane South	36	EC	G
		Rath-Healy	65		Military G
24M	Clonfert	Clonfert	22		G
		Coolacoosane	23		G
		Kanturk, Chapel Lane	23	RC	
		Strand Street		EC	G
		Knockduff Upper	5,14	RC	
		Lismire	15	RC	
		Newmarket, Island Lane	14,22	RC	
		Main Street		EC	G
		Tooreennagrena	4,13	RC	
25M	Clonmeen	Banteer	31	RC	
		Clonmeen North	31	EC	G
31E	Clonmel	Ballyvoloon	87		G
		Town of Queenstown, Spy Hill	87	Nunnery Chapel	
32E	Clonmult	Ballyeightragh	55		G
		Clonmult	54,55	RC	

NGA No.	CIVIL PARISH	TOWNLAND OR TOWN, STREET	OS No.	CHURCH	GRAVE-YARD
33E	Clonpriest	Clonpriest East	78		G
		Gortaroo	67	RC	
		Inchiquin	67,78	EC	
26M	Clontead	Milledunny	112	RC	
		Serehaneroe	112		G
34E	Cloyne	Ballycottin	89	EC	
		Cloyne, Church Street	88	EC	G
		Spittle Lane		RC	
35E	Coole	Coole Upper	36		G
				RC	
27M	Cooliney	Cooliney	7		G
28M	Corbally	Corbally	85		G
29M	Corcomohide				
36E	Corkbeg	Corkbeg	87,88	EC	G
	CORK CITY				
37E	Holy Trinity	Brunswick Street	74	Augustinian RC	
		Charlotte Quay		Capuchin RC	
		Georges Street		I	
		Main Street South		EC	
					G
		Marlboro Street		BAP	
		Princes Street		P	
		Queen Street		P	
				CB	
98E	St. Anne's Shandon	Black Millers Lane	74		Military G
		Clarence Street		RC	
		Glanmire Road Lower		RC	
		Great Britain Street		M	
		Military Road		M	
		Peacock Lane		RC	
		Phillpots Lane		St.Annes EC	
		Rogerson's Lane		St.Marys RC	

NGA No.	CIVIL PARISH	TOWNLAND OR TOWN, STREET	OS No.	CHURCH	GRAVE-YARD
98E	St. Anne's Shandon	St. Annes Church Yard	74	St.Annes EC	
		Summer-Hill		St.Lukes EC	
99E	St. Finbar's	Church Walk	74	St. Finbars EC	G
91M	St. Mary's Shandon	Pope's Quay	74	St,Marys RC	
		Shandon Street		St.Marys Shandon EC	G
		Sundays Well Road		RC Unfini-shed	
38E	St.Nicholas	Blackmoor Lane	74	RC	
		Blackrock Road		EC	
		Douglas Street		RC	G
				Monastery	G
					St.John's G
		Dunbar Street		South RC	
		Infirmary Road		EC	
		Quaker's Road			G
		Stephen's Street			G
		St. Nicholas' Church Lane		St. Nicholas' EC	G
		Tory-Top-Lane			St. Josephs G
39E	St. Paul's	Careys Lane	74	RC	
		French Church Street		M	
		Patrick Street		M	
		Paul Street		EC	G
40E	St. Peter's	Duncan Street	74	St. Francis RC	G
				Q	
		Fishamble Lane		St. Francis RC	

NGA No.	CIVIL PARISH	TOWNLAND OR TOWN, STREET	OS No.	CHURCH	GRAVE-YARD
40E	St. Peter's	Henry Street	74	M	
		North Main Street		St.Peters EC	
10W	Creagh	Creagh	141,150	EC	G
		Town of Skibbereen	141,142	RC	
		Skibbereen, Chapel Lane	141,142		G
					G
30M and 41E	Cullen	Cullen	98	EC	
					G
		Mullaghroe North	29	RC	G
31M	Currykippane	Clogheen	73,74	RC	
		Mount Desert	73,74		G
42E	Dangandonovan	Kilcounty	55,66		G
43E	Derryvillane	Derryvillane	18,19, 27		G
32M	Desert				
33M	Desertmore	Kilcrea	84		G
34M	Desertserges	Aghyohil More	109	RC	
		Knockmacool	109	EC	G
35M	Donaghmore	Coollicka	50,61		G
				RC	
		Coolmona	50	EC	
		Farnaght	50,61	RC	
		Lackabane	50,61		G
44E	Doneraile	Doneraile, Buttevant Lane	17,25	Convent Chapel	
		Main Street		RC	
		Garryhintoge	17,18		G
		Horseclose	17	EC	
		Oldcourt	17		G
11W	Drinagh	Driminidy North	133		G
		Drinagh West	120	EC	G
		Paddock	120	RC	
36M	Drishane	Millstreet, Main Street	39	RC	
				EC	

NGA No.	CIVIL PARISH	TOWNLAND OR TOWN, STREET	OS No.	CHURCH	GRAVE- YARD
12W	Dromdaleague	Dromdaleague	119,120	RC	
				EC	G
37M	Dromdowney				
38M	Dromtarriff	Dernagree	30	RC	
		Dromagh	30,31	RC	
				EC	
		Dromtarriff	30,31		G
		Garraveasoge	23,31		G
45E	Dunbulloge	Carrignavar	52,63	EC	
		Doonpeter	43		G
		Dunbulloge	52,63		G
		Laharan	52	RC	
39M	Dunderrow	Horsehill More North	111	EC	
					G
		Skehanagh	97	Chapel	G
46E	Dungourney	Dungourney	66	RC	
		Glebe	66	EC	G
40M	Dunisky	Dunisky	83,91		G
47E	Dunmahon	Dunmahon	27		G
13W	Durrus	Carrigboy	130,131	EC	G
				RC	
		Killoveenoge	117		G
		Murreagh	130,131	M	
14W	Fanlobbus	Town of Dumanway, Main Street	108	RC	G
				EC	G
				M	
		Kilbarry	107,120		G
		Nedinagh East	108		G
		Togher	93	RC	
48E	Farahy	Farahy	18	EC	G
49E	Fermoy	Carrignagroghera	35		G
		Fermoy, Allen's Walk	35	P	
		Artillery Quay		RC	

NGA No.	CIVIL PARISH	TOWNLAND OR TOWN, STREET	OS No.	CHURCH	GRAVE-YARD
49E	Fermoy	Fermoy, Barrack Street	35	EC	
		Chapel Square		RC	
		Walkers Row		M	
50E	Garranekinnefeake	Garranekinnefeake	76,88	EC	
		Jamesbrook	88		G
		Village of Scartlea, Middleton Road	88	RC	
41M	Garrycloyne	Ballygibbon	62	RC	
		Knocknalyre	62		G
51E	Garryvoe	Garryvoe Lower	77,89		G
52E	Glanworth	Boherash	27	EC	G
		Town of Glanworth, Chapel Lane	27	RC	
53E	Gortroe	Ballinterry	44		G
		Desert	45,54		G
		Garryantaggart	44,53	RC	
42M	Grenagh	Grenagh North	51	RC	
					G
43M	Hackmys				
54E	Ightermurragh	Ightermurragh	77	EC	G
		Knockglass	77	RC	
44M	Imphrick	Imphrick	7,8		G
55E	Inch	Inch	100	EC	G
15W	Inchigeelagh	Carrigleigh	81	RC	
		Dromanallig	80,81	RC	
		Glebe	81,82	EC	G
56E	Inchinabacky	Churchtown	76		G
				EC	
45M	Inishannon	Farnahoe	97	RC	G
		Inishannon, Main Street	97	EC	G
		Old Cork Road		M	
46M	Inishcarra	Carrigyknaveen	73	EC	
		Currabetha	73	RC	
		Garravagh	61		G
		Gortray	61	RC	

NGA No.	CIVIL PARISH	TOWNLAND OR TOWN, STREET	OS No.	CHURCH	GRAVE-YARD
46M	Inishcarra	Kilmurry	61		G
47M	Inishkenny	Inishkenny	85	EC	G
16W	Island				
48M	Kilbolane	Village of Milford	1	RC	
				EC	G
		Shronepookeen	1,6	RC	
49M	Kilbonane	Kilbonane	84		G
		Rathard	84	EC	
50M	Kilbrin	Bawnmore North	15		G
		Castlecor Demesne	23,24		G
		Knockballymartin	15,16, 23,24	RC	
		Lackeel	16	EC	G
51M	Kilbrittain	Kilbrittain	123,124		G
52M	Kilbrogan	Bandon, Barrett's Hill	110	RC	
		North Main Street		EC	
		Watergate Street		P	
		Kilbrogan	96,110	Chapel	
53M	Kilbroney	Kilbroney	16,17		G
17W	Kilcaskan	Ballynakilla	103		Childrens G
		Cappyaughna	90,104	RC	G
		Drumlave	116	RC	
		Furkeal	104		Childrens G
18W	Kilcatherine	Ardgroom Inward	102	EC	
		Village of Eyeries	102,114	RC	
		Gortgarriff	101		G
19W	Kilcoe	Corravoley	140	EC	
		Kilcoe	140	RC	
					G
54M	Kilcorcoran	Rossline	15,23		G
55M	Kilcorney	Kilcorney	39		G
		Shanakill	39,40	RC	
57E	Kilcredan	Kilcredan	77,78	EC	G

NGA No.	CIVIL PARISH	TOWNLAND OR TOWN, STREET	OS No.	CHURCH	GRAVE-YARD
20W	Kilcrohane	Kilcrohane	129,138	RC	
					G
		Rosnacaheragh	130	RC	
58E	Kilcrumper	Lisnasallagh	27,35		G
59E	Kilcully	Kilcully	60	EC	G
60E	Kilcummer	Kilcummer Lower	26,34		G
61E	Kildorrery	Village of Kildorrery	18		G
				RC	
21W	Kilfaughnabeg				
22W	Kilgarriff	Clonakilty, Barrack Street	135	EC	G
		Boyle Street		M	
		New Chapel Street		RC	
		Kilgarriff	122,135		G
56M	Kilgrogan	Kilgrogan	7		G
62E	Kilgullane	Kilgullane	19		G
23W	Kilkerranmore	Belad West	121,134	RC	
		Creagh Beg	135	RC	
		Gortnascarty	135		G
24W	Killaconenagh	Ballynakilla	115,128	RC	G
		Castletown Bearhaven	115	EC	
				RC	
		Cloonaghlin West	128		G
		Curradonohoe	115		G
		Curryglass	115	RC	
		Rodeen	115		G
63E	Killanully	Killanully	86		G
64E	Killaspugmullane	Coolnacha	64		G
65E	Killathy	Killathy	27,35		G
66E	Killeagh	Town of Killeagh, Main Street	66	RC	
				EC	G
67E	Killeenemer				
57M	Killowen	Killowen	95,109		G
				EC	

COUNTY CORK

NGA No.	CIVIL PARISH	TOWNLAND OR TOWN, STREET	OS No.	CHURCH	GRAVE- YARD
25W	Kilmacabea	Kilmacabea	133,142		G
				RC	
				EC	
68E	Kilmacdonogh	Ballymacoda	78		G
		Village of Ballymacoda	78	RC	
58M	Kilmaclenine	Kilmaclenine	24		G
69E	Kilmahon	Shangarry South	89	EC	G
				RC	
59M	Kilmaloda	Clogagh North	123	RC	
		Clogagh South	123		G
		Kilmaloda	122,123	EC	G
60M	Kilmeen	Ballyhoolahan East	22		G
		Village of Boherboy	22	RC	
		Kishkeam Lower	21	RC	
26W	Kilmeen	Glebe	121	EC	G
		Kilmeen	121	Part of RC	
		Rossmore	121	Part of RC	
27W	Kilmichael	Cooldorragha	82	RC	
		Johnstown	82,94	RC	
		Moneycusker	82	EC	G
28W	Kilmocomoge	Abbey	118		G
		Bantry, Moarin's Street	118	EC	
		Mill Street		M	
		Carrignagat	118	RC	
		Cooryleary	105	RC	
		Dromdoneen	105,118	EC	
		Dromkeal	105	EC	
		Kealkill	92,106	RC	
		Lisheen	105,106		G
29W	Kilmoe	Altar	147,148	EC	
		Boulysallagh	147	RC	
		Crookhaven	147,152	EC	G

53

COUNTY CORK

NGA No.	CIVIL PARISH	TOWNLAND OR TOWN, STREET	OS No.	CHURCH	GRAVE-YARD
29W	Kilmoe	Goleen	147	RC in Progress EC	G
		Lissagriffin	147		G
70E	Kilmoney	Village of Carrigaline, Main Street	87,99	RC	
71E	Kilmonoge	Coolnagaug	112		G
61M	Kilmurry	Coolduff	83	RC EC	G
62M	Kilnaglory	Ballynora	73,85	RC	
		Kilnaglory	73,85		G
63M	Kilnagross	Beanhill South	122	EC	G
30W	Kilnamanagh	Ballaghboy	126		G
		Cloan	114	RC	G
		Kilkinnikin West	127	RC	
		Loughanibey	127		G
31W	Kilnamartery	Ballyvoge	70	RC	
		Glebe	70	EC	G
72E	Kilpatrick	Kilpatrick	99		G
73E	Kilphelan	Kilphelan	19		G
74E	Kilquane	Kilquane	64		G
		Village of Knockraha	64	RC	
		Mitchellsfort	53	EC	
64M	Kilquane				
65M	Kilroan	Courtaparteen	124,125		G
66M	Kilroe				
75E	Kilshanahan	Ballinaltig	44,53		G
67M	Kilshannig	Beennamweel East	51,50	RC	
		Brittas	32,41	RC	
		Kilgobnet	41		G
		Kilpadder South	32,41	RC	
		Newberry	32	EC	G

NGA No.	CIVIL PARISH	TOWNLAND OR TOWN, STREET	OS No.	CHURCH	GRAVE-YARD
68M	Kilsillagh				
76E	Kilworth	Glansheskin	28	RC	G
		Village of Kilworth, Main Street	27,28	EC	G
32W	Kinneigh	Castletown	95	RC	
		Derrigra	109	RC	
		Rushfield	95	M	
		Sleenoge	94	EC	G
69M	Kinsale	Kinsale, Church Street	112,125	EC	G
		Friars Street		RC	
				RC	
		Higher Street		M	
		Lower Catholic Walk		RC	
		Main Street		M	
		Newmans Mall		RC	
		Rampart		RC	
77E	Kinure	Kinure	112,125		G
70M	Knockavilly	Kill	84,85, 96,97		G
				EC	
		Russelhill	84,85, 96,97	RC	
78E	Knockmourne	Conna	45,46	RC	
		Curraheen	37,46	EC	G
		Glebe	45		G
71M	Knocktemple	Village of Freemount	6,15	RC	
		Knawhill	6,7		G
72M	Lackeen	Lackeen	7,16		G
73M	Leighmoney	Leighmoney	111		G
79E	Leitrim	Ballynalacken	28,36		G
74M	Liscarroll	Village of Liscarroll, Main Street	15,16	RC	
					G
80E	Liscleary	Meadstown	86,98		G
81E	Lisgoold	Leamlara	64	RC	

NGA No.	CIVIL PARISH	TOWNLAND OR TOWN, STREET	OS No.	CHURCH	GRAVE- YARD
81E	Lisgoold	Lisgoold East	65	EC	G
				RC	
75M	Lislee	Village of Butlerstown	136	RC	
		Town of Courtmacsherry	136	RC	
		Lisleetemple	136	EC	G
82E	Lismore and Mocollop				
83E	Litter	Castlehyde East	35	EC	G
84E	Little Island	Wallingstown	75		G
76M	Macloneigh	Tooms West	70,71, 82,85	RC	
85E	Macroney	Coolmoohan	28	RC	
		Macroney Lower	28		G
77M	Macroom	Ballynagree West	49,50	RC	
		Macroom, Castle Street	71	EC	G
		Chapel Lane		RC	
78M	Magourney	Glebe	72	EC	G
		Kilcolman	61		G
		Nadrid	72	RC	
79M	Mallow	Mallow, Fair Lane	33	Z	
		Main Street		RC	G
				M	
				EC	G
		New Street		M	
86E	Marmullane	Ardmore	75,87		G
		Passage West, Chapel Street	75,87	RC	
		Church Lane		EC	
		Wesley Place		M	
87E	Marshalstown	Killaclug West	10,19	RC	
		Marshalstown	18	EC	G
80M	Matehy	Gilcagh	62	RC	
88E	Middleton	Ballynacorra	76		G
		Broomfield West	65,76		G
		Middleton, Chapel Road	76	RC	
		Church Lane		EC	G

NGA No.	CIVIL PARISH	TOWNLAND OR TOWN, STREET	OS No.	CHURCH	GRAVE-YARD
88E	Middleton	Middleton, Main Street	76	RC	
89E	Mogeely	Town of Castlemartyr, Main Street	77	EC	G
		Glengoura Lower	46	RC	
		Mogeely	66	RC	
					G
		Mogeely Lower	37,46		G
		Rosybower	37,46	EC	G
		Templevalley	46		G
90E	Mogeesha	Ballyvodock West	76	EC	
91E	Monanimy	Ballymagmoy	33,34	RC	
		Monanimy Lower	34	EC	G
92E	Monkstown	Monkstown, Creek Kernan Cottages	87		G
		Glen Road		EC	
81M	Mourneabbey	Ballynamona	42	EC	
		Burnfort	42	RC (Old) RC (New)	
		Garrynagearagh	42	RC	
		Kilquane	42		G
82M	Moviddy	Bellmount Lower	83,84	EC	G
		Coolmucky	84	RC	
83M	Murragh	Coolanagh	95	RC	
		Farranthomas	95	EC	
33W	Myross	Brade	142		G
		Clontaff	142	RC	
		Listarkin	142	EC	
		Myross	142,151		G
93E	Nohaval	Village of Nohaval	112,113	EC RC	G
84M	Nohavaldaly	Farrankeal	29	RC	
		Nohaval Lower	28,29		G
94E	Rahan	Ballymagooly	33	EC	G
		Dromrahan	33		G

NGA No.	CIVIL PARISH	TOWNLAND OR TOWN, STREET	OS No.	CHURCH	GRAVE-YARD
34W	Rathbarry	Castlefreke	143	EC	
		Milltown	134,143, 144	RC	
85M	Rathclarin	Farrannagark	123	EC	G
		Glanduff	123,124	RC	
95E	Rathcooney	Village of Glanmire	63,64, 74,75	EC	
		Rathcooney	63		G
		Village of Sallybrook	63	RC	
96E	Rathcormack	Kildinan	44		G
		Village of Rathcormack, Dispensary Lane	44	M	
		Main Street		RC	
				EC	G
86M	Rathgoggan	Charleville, Clancy Street	2,3	RC	
		Main Street		Z	
				EC	G
		Rathgoggan South	2,3		G
87M	Ringcurran	Ardbrack	112	EC	G
		Forthill	112,125		G
88M	Ringrone	Ballinspittle	124	RC	
		Castlelands	125		G
		Oldcourt	124	EC	
35W	Ross	Ardagh East	134,143	RC	
		Knocknageehy	134,143		G
		Town of Ross Carberry	143	EC	G
89M	Rosskeen				
97E	Rostellan	Ballinrostig	88	RC	
98E	St. Anne's Shandon	Farranferris	74	RC	
90M	St. Finbar's	Ballintemple	74		G
		Ballinure	74,75	RC	
		Curraghconway	86,87	EC	G
		Dundanion	74	RC	
				EC	G
100E	St. Michael's	Ballinvriskig	63	RC	

NGA No.	CIVIL PARISH	TOWNLAND OR TOWN, STREET	OS No.	CHURCH	GRAVE-YARD
101E	St. Nathlash	Village of Rockmills, Main Street	18,26	EC	G
93M	Shandrum	Ballynakilla East	2	RC	
		Village of Dromina	6,7	RC	
		Killabraher South	7		G
		Killaree	2	EC	
36W	Skull	Arderrawinny	139,148	RC	
		Town of Ballydehob, Chapel Lane	140	RC M	
		Cooragurteen	140	EC	
		Dunbeacon	130,139	RC	
		Lissacaha	139	M	
		Skull	139,148	EC	G
		Town of Skull, Main Street	139,148	RC M	
94M	Subutler				
102E	Templebodan	Templebodan	54		G
103E	Templebreedy	Kilcolta	99	EC	G
		Myrtleville	99	RC	
95M	Templebryan				
96M	Templemartin	Farranhavane	96	RC	
		Garranes	84,96	EC	
97M	Templemichael	Clogheenduane	97	EC	G
104E	Templemolaga	Knocknevin	10,19	RC	
		Labbamolaga Middle	10		G
105E	Templenacarriga	Templenacarriga North	65	EC	G
98M	Templeomalus	Ballintemple	135	EC	G
		Darrary	135	RC	
99M	Templequinlan	Cloghgriffen	135,136		G
106E	Templeroan	Clogher Demesne	18,26		G
		Village of Shanballymore, Main Street	18	RC	
107E	Templerobin	Ballymore	87,88	RC	G

NGA No.	CIVIL PARISH	TOWNLAND OR TOWN, STREET	OS No.	CHURCH	GRAVE-YARD
107E	Templerobin	Queenstown, Church Hill	87	M	
				EC	
		East Beach		P	
100M	Templetrine	Currarane	124		G
		Kilmore		EC	G
108E	Templeusque	Templeusque	63		G
101M	Timoleague	Castle Lower	123	EC	G
		Timoleague, Abbey Street	123,136	Abbey Ruins	G
		Chapel Road		RC	
102M	Tisaxon	Tisaxon Beg	111		G
109E	Titeskin				
110E	Trabolgan				
111E	Tracton	Laharran	99,113	RC	
		Tubbrid	98,99	EC	G
37W	Tullagh	Baltimore	149,150		G
				EC	
		Kilmoon	149,153	RC	
		Rathmore	150	RC	
103M	Tullylease	Tullylease	6		G
				RC	
112E	Wallstown	Wallstown	18,26	EC	G
104M	Whitechurch	Whitechurch	52,63	RC	
				EC	G
113E	Youghal	Youghal Lands	67	RC	
		Youghal, Bean Street	67	RC	
				Q	G
		Meeting House Lane		M	
				I	
		Nelson Place		St.Mary's RC	
					G
		Old Chapel Lane			G
		South Abbey		EC	
				RC	
		South Main Street		M	

NGA No.	CIVIL PARISH	TOWNLAND OR TOWN, STREET	OS No.	CHURCH	GRAVE- YARD
1	Aghanunshin	Cornagill	53	EC	
		Kiltoy	53		G
2	All Saints	Colehill	46	EC	G
				RC	G
		Garshooey	55	P	G
		Newtowncunningham	46,54	P	G
3	Aughnish	Glenalla	28,37	EC in progress	
		Kilcreen	46	RC	
		Killydonnell	46		G
		Rathmelton, Back Lane	45,46	P	
				M	
		Church Street		EC in ruins	G
				EC	
		Tank Road		P	
4	Burt	Carrownamaddy	47	P	
		Castlecooly	47	EC	
		Drumhaggart	38,39		G
		Speenoge	47	RC	
5	Clonca	Ballygorman	2	RC	
		Clonca	4,5,11,12		G
		Dunross	4,5,12	RC	
		Goorey	4	P	
		Lag	4	RC	G
		Malin, The Green	4	EC	
		Templemoyle	4		G
				RC	G
6	Clondahorky	Ballymore Lower	16,26	EC	
					G
		Cashelmore	26	RC	G
		Castledoe	26		G
		Clonbeg Glebe	26		G
		Derryart	26	P	
		Kill	15,16		G

NGA No.	CIVIL PARISH	TOWNLAND OR TOWN, STREET	OS No.	CHURCH	GRAVE-YARD
6	Clondahorky	Kill	15,16		G
7	Clondavaddog	Croaghan	17	RC	G
		Fanavolty	8	RC	
		Rosnakill	17	EC	
		Tirlaydan	28	RC	
8	Clonleigh	Village of Ballindrait	70	P	
		Edenmore	71	G	
		Lifford Common	70	RC	
		Lifford, Main Street	71	EC	G
9	Clonmany	Clehagh	10	RC	G
		Straid	10,19	EC	G
10	Convoy	Ballyboe	69	COV	G
		Convoy, Main Street	69	EC	G
				P	
				RC	
		Drumkeen	69	RC	G
11	Conwal	Carnatreantagh	44	P	
		Conwal	53		G
		Gortlee	53	COV	
		Kilpheak	52	RC	
		Letterkenny	53	P	
		Letterkenny, Church Lane	53	EC	G
				P	
				RC	
		Main Street		RC	
				2nd P	
		Market Square		M	
		Templedouglas	52		G
12	Culdaff	Aghaglassan	11,12, 20,21	EC	
		Culdaff	5		G
		Town of Culdaff	5	EC	G
13	Desertegny	Gortleck	18,19	RC	
		Linsfort	18,19, 28,29	EC	G

NGA No.	CIVIL PARISH	TOWNLAND OR TOWN, STREET	OS No.	CHURCH	GRAVE-YARD
14	Donagh	Carndonagh, Bridge Street	4,11,20	M	
		Chapel Street		EC	G
				RC	G
		Tullanree	11	P	G
15	Donaghmore	Ballymacor	78	RC	G
				RC	
		Carowen	69,70, 79	SP	G
		Carricknashane	79	P	
		Castlefinn	79	RC	G
		Town of Castlefin	79	M	
		Donaghmore Glebe	79	EC	G
		Dromore	78	EC	G
		Sessiagh O'Neill	78	RC	G
16	Donegal	Donegal, Bridge Street	93,94	EC	
		Main Street		RC	
				Z	
		Glebe	93,99		G
		Spierstown	94	RC	G
17	Drumhome	Ballintra, Grahamstown Road	103	M	
		Main Street		EC	
		Killinangel Beg	103	EC	
		Village of Laghy	100	EC	G
		Lismintan on Ballyruddelly	103	RC	
		Mullanacross	99,103		G
					G
		Raneany West	100	P	
18	Fahan Lower	Ballymacarry	29	RC	
					G
		Buncrana, William Street	29	P	
				EC	G
19	Fahan Upper	Carrowmullin	38	EC	
		Castlequarter	38	RC	G
		Glebe	38		G

NGA No.	CIVIL PARISH	TOWNLAND OR TOWN, STREET	OS No.	CHURCH	GRAVE-YARD
19	Fahan Upper	Tievebane	38	P	
20	Gartan	Ballymaquin	52	RC	
		Church Hill	44,52	EC	G
		Churchtown	44		G
21	Glencolumbkille	Cashel	80,89, 90	RC	
		Straid or Glebe	80	EC	G
22	Inch	Carnaghan	37,38	P RC	
		Grange	37,38		G
		Moress	38	EC	
23	Inishkeel	Drumnasillagh	74,75		G
		Fintown	56,66 67	RC	G
		Town of Glenties	74,75	RC	
		Gortnamucklagh	74	EC	
		Islands	64,65		G
		Kilclooney More	64,73	RC in progress	G
		Kilkenny	65		G
		Naran	64	EC	
24	Inishmacsaint	Town of Ballyshannon (The West Rock)	107	RC	G
		Town of Bundoran	106,109	M	
		Finner	106,107		G
		Magheracar	106,109	EC RC in progress	
25	Inver	Cranny Lower	92,93	EC	G
		Drumard	93	RC	G
26	Kilbarron	Abbey Island	107		G
		Ballyshannon, Chapel Lane	107	RC	
		Church Lane		EC	G
		Main Street Upper		M	
		The Mall		M	

NGA No.	CIVIL PARISH	TOWNLAND OR TOWN, STREET	OS No.	CHURCH	GRAVE-YARD
26	Kilbarron	Carricknahorna	107,108	Preaching house	
		Cashelard	103,104 107,108	RC	
		Clough	107,108		G
		Sminver	107		G
		Townparks	107	P	G
27	Kilcar	Town of Kilcar	96	RC	
		Newchurch Glebe	96	EC EC	G
28	Killaghtee	Ballyederlan	98	M	
		Beaugreen Glebe	98	EC	G
		Bruckless	98	RC	
		Dunkineely, Main Street	98	M	
29	Killea	Town of Carrigans	55	EC	
30	Killybegs Lower	Ardara, Main Street	73,74, 82	M RC	G
		Kilrean Upper	74		G
		Mullanacloy	82,83		G
31	Killybegs Upper	Corporation	91,97	EC	
		Glebe	97		G
		Killybegs, Chapel Road	91,97	RC RC	
		Fair Hill		Old RC	
32	Killygarvan	Legland	28,37	RC	
		Rathmullan, Church Hill	37	EC	G
		Kerrs Bay Road		P	G
		Wesleyan Street		M	
33	Killymard	Ballydevitt	93	EC	
		Donegal, New Road	93	M P	
		Eddrim Glebe	93		G
		Haugh	93,94	RC	

NGA No.	CIVIL PARISH	TOWNLAND OR TOWN, STREET	OS No.	CHURCH	GRAVE-YARD
33	Killymard	Lougheask Demesne	94	EC	
34	Kilmacrenan	Cashel	26	EC	G
		Kilconnell or Glebe	45	EC	
		Village of Kilmacrenan	45	EC in ruins	G G
		Knocknabollan	35,44	RC	
		Letter	45	P	
		Massreagh	45	RC	
35	Kilteevoge	Glebe	68	EC	G
		Kiltyfergal	68,77	RC	
36	Leck	Drumany	53,61	EC	
37	Lettermacaward	Madavagh	65	RC	
		Meenagowan	65	EC	G
38	Mevagh	Carrickart	17,27	EC P	G
		Clontallagh	16		G
		Umlagh	16,17, 26,27	RC	G
39	Mintiaghs or Barr of Inch				
40	Moville Lower	Ballybrack	13,22	RC	G
		Carrowblagh or Leckenny	12	RC	
		Carrowhugh	13,22		G
		Drumaweer	13,22	EC	
		Town of Moville	12,13, 21,22	Site of new EC	
41	Moville Upper	Clare	21	P	
		Cooly	12,21		G
		Drung	20,21, 30,31	RC	
		Tullynavinn	21,23	EC	
42	Muff	Derryvane	39	P	
		Eskaheen	30,39	RC	G
		Muff	39	EC	G
43	Raphoe	Raphoe, The Diamond	70	P	G
		Meeting House Street		P	G

NGA No.	CIVIL PARISH	TOWNLAND OR TOWN, STREET	OS No.	CHURCH	GRAVE-YARD
44	Raymoghy	Balleeghan	54		G
		Drumoghill	54,62	RC	
		Errity	54	SP	G
		Manorcunningham	54	P	
		Raymoghy	54	EC	G
					G
45	Raymunterdoney	Moyra Glebe	25,34	EC	
		Ray	25,34		G
46	Stranorlar	Drumboe Lower	78	M	
		Glebe	78	EC	G
		Stranorlar	78	M	
			78	Site of RC	
		Stranorlar, Chapel Lane	78	RC	G
		Meeting House Lane		P	
47	Taughboyne	Ballylennan	62	P	
		Clashy	54,55, 63	RC	
		Haw	55	EC	G
		Listannagh	62	P	
		Town of Saint Johnstown	63		G
				RC in progress	
				P	
		Tonagh	55	P	
48	Templecarn	Carn	101,105		G
		Cashelenny	102	EC	
		Lettercran	102	RC	
		Pettigoe	105	RC	
		Pettigoe, Main Street	105	EC	
		Station Island (Lough Derg)	101	St. Patricks RC	
				St.Marys RC	
49	Templecrone	Belcruit	41	RC	G
		Dunglow	49	RC in progress	G

NGA No.	CIVIL PARISH	TOWNLAND OR TOWN, STREET	OS No.	CHURCH	GRAVE-YARD
49	Templecrone	Gortgarra	40,48		G
		Illion	40,48	RC	
		Meenmore	48,49	EC	G
50	Tullaghobegley	Ballintemple	25		G
		Derrybeg	32	RC	
		Dunlewy Near	42,43	EC	
		Gortahork	24	RC	
		Killult	24	EC	
		Magheracallan	32		G
		Magheraclogher	32	EC	
		Tory Island	6		G
51	Tullyfern	Bridge End or Drummonaghan	45	COV	
		Carrowkeel	27,28	P	
		Loughros Glebe	36	RC	
		Millford, Church Street	36	COV	
		Rossreagh	45,46	P	
		Tullymore	45		G
52	Urney	Alt Upper	79,88	P	
		Dunnaloob	79	RC	G

NGA No.	CIVIL PARISH	TOWNLAND OR TOWN, STREET	OS No.	CHURCH	GRAVE-YARD
1	Aghaderg	Caskum	34	P	G
		Glaskermore	41	P	G
		Lisnagade	33	RC	G
		Town of Loughbrickland	33,34		G
				RC	
				EC	G
				M	
				P	
		Village of Scarva	33	P	
				EC	G
2	Annaclone	Ardbrin	34,65		G
		Ballydown	27,34	P	G
		Ballynanny	34	P	
		Lisnasliggan	34	EC	G
		Tullintanvally	34	RC	G
				P	G
3	Annahilt	Cargacreevy	15,22	P	G
		Cargygary	22	P	G
		Glebe	·22	EC	G
4	Ardglass	Ardglass, High Street	45	RC	
		Hill Street		M	
		Kildare Street		P	
				EC	G
5	Ardkeen	Ardkeen	25		G
		Kirkistown	18,25	EC	G
		Lisbane	25	RC	
6	Ardquin	Ardquin	24,25	EC	G
7	Ballee	Ballycruttle	38	RC	G
		Ballyhosset Milltown	38,45	P	
		Church Ballee	38	P	
				EC	G
8	Ballyculter	Ballyculter Upper	31	EC	G
		Cargagh	38	RC	
		Strangford Lower	31,32	EC	G

NGA No.	CIVIL PARISH	TOWNLAND OR TOWN, STREET	OS No.	CHURCH	GRAVE-YARD
8	Ballyculter	Town of Strangford	31,32	P	G
				M	
				RC	G
				M	
9	Ballyhalbert Alias St. Andrew	Ballyesborough	18	EC	G
		Ballyhalbert	18		G
		Ballyhemlin	18	P	G
		Glastry	18	P	G
				M	
10	Ballykinler	Ballykinler Upper	44		Old G
11	Ballyphilip	Ballygalget	32	RC	
		Portaferry, Church Street	32	EC	
					G
		Ferry Street		M	
		Meeting House Lane		M	
				P	
12	Ballytrustan	Ballytrustan	32		G
13	Ballywalter	Ballywalter	12	P	
		Village of Ballywalter	12	P	
		Whitechurch	12	EC	
					G
14	Bangor	Ballygilbert	1	P	
		Ballygrainey	2,6	P	
		Bangor, Main Street	2	P	
		Sandy Row		M	
		Village of Conlig	2,6	P	G
				BAP	
		Corporation	2	RC	
				P	
				EC	G
		Groomsport	2	EC	
		Groomsport, Main Street	2	P	

NGA No.	CIVIL PARISH	TOWNLAND OR TOWN, STREET	OS No.	CHURCH	GRAVE-YARD
15	Blaris	Annacloy	14	M	
		Blaris	14		G
		Maze	14	P	
16	Bright	Bright	45	EC	G
		Coniamstown	37,38, 44,45	RC	
		Legamaddy	37,44, 45	RC in progress	G
17	Castleboy	Cloghy	25	P	
18	Clonallan	Burren	51	RC	G
		Clonallan Glebe	51,54	EC	G
		Mayo	47,51	RC	G
19	Clonduff	Ballyaughian	48,52		G
		Ballygorian Beg	47,48	RC	G
		Ballymaghery	48	RC	G
		Ballynagappoge	42	P	G
		Cabragh	42	RC	G
		Town of Hilltown	48	EC	G
				P	G
20	Comber	Comber, Bridge Street	10	M	
		The Crescent		RC	
		High Street		1st P	
		Market Street		2nd P	
		Mill Street		U	
		The Square		EC	G
		Gransha	10	P	G
		Moneyreagh	10	U	G
21	Donaghadee	Ballycopeland	6,7	P	G
		Ballyfrenis	6,7	P	
		Ballymacruise	7	P	G
		Ballyrawer	6,7	EC	G
				P	
		Donaghadee, Church Lane	2,3	EC	G

COUNTY DOWN

NGA No.	CIVIL PARISH	TOWNLAND OR TOWN, STREET	OS No.	CHURCH	GRAVE-YARD
21	Donaghadee	Donaghadee, High Street	2,3	RC	
				P	
		Mount Street		M	
		Warren Road		P	
		Drumfad	7		G
		Miller Hill	7		G
22	Donaghcloney	Ballynabragget	20,27	P	
		Donaghcloney	20		G
		Tullyherron	19,20	P	
		Village of Waringstown	19,20	EC	G
23	Donaghmore	Ballyblaugh	40	RC	
				RC in progress	
		Ballymacaratty More	33,40	P	G
		Cargabane	41	M	
		Carrickrovaddy	40,46	RC	
		Glebe	40,41	EC	G
24	Down	Ballykilbeg	37	RC	
		Ballyrolly	37		G
		Demesne of Down	30,31, 37,38		Workhouse G
		Downpatrick, Bridge Street	37	UP	
		Church Lane		M	
				EC	G
		English Street		EC	G
		Fountain Street		P	
					G
		Irish Street		Convent Chapel	
		Scotch Street		M	
		Stream Street		RC	G
				U	G
		Hollymount	37	EC	
25	Dromara	Ardtanagh	28	1st P	G
		Begny	28,29	M	

NGA No.	CIVIL PARISH	TOWNLAND OR TOWN, STREET	OS No.	CHURCH	GRAVE-YARD
25	Dromara	Dromara	28	EC	G
		Town of Dromara	28	P	
		Dunmore	29,36	RC	
		Enagh	28	P	G
		Finnis	28,35	RC	G
26	Dromore	Balleny	20,21, 27,28	A	G
				P	
		Dromore, Brewery Lane	21	COV	
		Church Street		EC	G
		Hillsborough Street		RC	G
		Wesley Place		M	
				M	
		Drumbroneth	20,21, 27,28	P	G
		Drumlough	21	P	
27	Drumballyroney	Aughnavollog	41,42	EC	G
		Ballooly	27,28	RC	
		Grallaghgreenan	41	P	
		Lackan	42	P	G
		Lisnavaghrog	35,41, 42	RC	G
		Rathfryland, Hawthorns Row	41	COV	G
28	Drumbeg	Drennan	15	P	G
		Drumbeg	9	EC	G
		Legacurry	14,15	P	
					G
29	Drumbo	Ballycarn	9	P	G
		Ballylessan	9	EC	G
		Ballynavally	9	M	
		Carryduff	9,15	P	G
		Drumbo	9,15	P	
30	Drumgath	Barnmeen	41,47	RC	G
		Drumgath	47		G
		Lurgancahone	41,47	RC	

NGA No.	CIVIL PARISH	TOWNLAND OR TOWN, STREET	OS No.	CHURCH	GRAVE-YARD
30	Drumgath	Rathfryland, Church Street	41	EC	
				M	
		Graveyard Land			G
		Newry Street		P	G
				RC	
				Q	
				P	
				P	
31	Drumgooland	Ballyward	35,42	EC	G
		Benraw	35,36	P	
		Cloghskelt	35	P	G
		Deehommed	35		G
				RC	G
		Derryneill	35,42	BAP in progress	
		Drumadonnell	35,42		G
		Drumlee	42	P	
		Gargarry	42	RC	
		Leitrim	35,36	RC	
32	Dundonald	Ballylisbredan	5	BA	
		Village of Dundonald	5	P	
				EC	G
33	Dunsfort	Balledock Upper	38,45	RC	G
		Dunsfort	38	EC	G
34	Garvaghy	Fedany	28	EC	G
		Kilkinamurray	28,35	P	G
35	Grey Abbey	Village of Grey Abbey	12	P	
				P	
		Rosemount	11,12	EC	
					G
36	Hillsborough	Ballykeel Artifinny	14,21	St. James EC	
		Ballykeel Edenagonnell	14,21	P	G
		Corcreeny	14,21	MO	G

NGA No.	CIVIL PARISH	TOWNLAND OR TOWN, STREET	OS No.	CHURCH	GRAVE-YARD
36	Hillsborough	Corcreeny	14,21	St. Johns EC	G
		Hillsborough, Lisburn Street	14	P	
		Main Street		EC	G
		Park Street			G
		Reillys Trench	14	RC	G
37	Holywood	Ballyrobert	1	EC	
		Holywood, Bangor Road	1	P	
		Church Lane Old			G
		Church Street		EC	
		Church View		RC	
		High Street		U	
				M	
				P	
		Morrows Lane		P	
		Strandtown	4	EC in progress	
38	Inch	Ballynacraig	30	EC	
		Inch	37		G
		Magheracranmoney	30	RC	
39	Inishargy	Balliggan	12,18	EC	G
		Kircubbin	18	P	G
		Town of Kircubbin	18	EC	
		Nuns Quarter	18	RC	
40	Kilbroney	Ballyedmond	54,55	RC	
		Kilbroney	51,52, 54		St.Brunos G
		Rosstrevor	54	RC	
				UP	
		Rosstrevor, Church Street	54		G
		Mary Street		P	
41	Kilclief	Ballywoodan	30,38	RC	
		Kilclief	38,39	EC	G
42	Kilcoo	Ballaghbeg	49	P	
				RC	G

NGA No.	CIVIL PARISH	TOWNLAND OR TOWN, STREET	OS No.	CHURCH	GRAVE-YARD
42	Kilcoo	Ballyhafry	43,49	RC	G
				EC	G
		Ballymoney	42		G
				RC	
					G
		Newcastle, Shore Road	49	M	
				EC	
		Slievenalargy	42,43	EC	
43	Kilkeel	Ballaghanery Upper	49,53		G
		Ballykeel	56		G
		Ballymageogh	52,55	RC	G
		Ballymartin	56	P	G
				RC	G
		Glasdrumman	53	RC	
		Kilkeel, Bridge Street	55,56		G
		Greencastle Street		P	G
		Meeting House Lane		P	
		Newcastle Street		MO	G
		Newry Street		EC	G
		Lisnacree	55		G
		Moneydorragh More	53,56	EC	G
				M	
				P	G
44	Killaney	Carrickmaddyroe	15	EC	G
				P	
				P	G
		Killaney	15,22		G
45	Killinchy	Balloo	16,17	P	G
		Ballygowan	16	P	G
		Ballymacashem	16	P	
		Carrickmannan	16	RC	
		Drumreagh	16		G
		Killinchy	17	EC	G
		Raffery	16,23	P	G

NGA No.	CIVIL PARISH	TOWNLAND OR TOWN, STREET	OS No.	CHURCH	GRAVE-YARD
45	Killinchey	Ravara	16	U	G
46	Killyleagh	Corporation	24,31		G
		Killyleagh, Church Hill Street	24	EC	G
		Cow Street		P	
		Irish Street		RC	
		The Plantation		P	G
		Shore Street		M	
		Toy and Kirkland	24		G
47	Kilmegan	Aghalasnafin	36,43	RC	G
		Castlewellan	43	EC	
		Town of Castlewellan	43	RC	
				P	
				M	
		Clonvaraghan	36,43	RC	G
		Moneylane	43,44	EC	G
48	Kilmood	Ballyministragh	16,17	P	
		Kilmood and Ballybunden	16,17	EC	G
49	Kilmore	Barnmaghery	23		G
		Carnacully	30	EC	G
		Crossgar, Downpatrick Street	30	RC	
		Drumaghlis	23,30	P	G
		Village of Kilmore	30	RC	
		Lissara	30	P	
		Rademan	23,30	U	G
50	Knockbreda	Breda	9	EC	G
		Castlereagh	4,9	P	G
		Gilnahirk	5,10	P	G
		Knock	4,5		G
		Knockbreckan	9	P	G
		Town of Newtownbreda	9	M	
51	Lambeg	Lisnatrunk	8,9, 14,15	P	
					G
52	Loughinisland	Town of Clough	37	1st P	G

NGA No.	CIVIL PARISH	TOWNLAND OR TOWN, STREET	OS No.	CHURCH	GRAVE-YARD
52	Loughinisland	Town of Clough	37	U	G
		Drumaroad	36	RC	G
		Naghan	37	P	
		Town of Seaforde	37	EC	G
		Tievenadarragh	30,37	RC	G
53	Maghera	Ballyginny	43	M	
		Carnacavill	43,49	EC	G
54	Magheradool	Ballymaglave North	22,29	P	
		Ballynahinch	22,29	EC	G
		Ballynahinch, Alfred Street	22	3rd P	
		Church Street		RC	
		Lisburn Street		M	
		Windmill Street		1st P	G
		Glassdrumman	22		G
		Magheradool	29	EC in ruins	G
55	Magherahamlet	Drumgavlin	29	EC P	
56	Magheralin	Ballymakeonan	13		G
		Ballynadrone	13	EC	
		Village of Magheralin	13	RC	
57	Magherally	Magherally	27	EC P	G G
58	Moira	Carnalbanagh East	13	P U	
		Clare	13	EC	
		Lurganville	13,20	RC	
		Town of Moira	13	M	
59	Newry	Finnard	41,47	P	G
		Greenan	50,51		G
		Lisserboy	40,41	P	G
		Newry, Chapel Street Upper	46,50	RC	G

NGA No.	CIVIL PARISH	TOWNLAND OR TOWN, STREET	OS No.	CHURCH	GRAVE-YARD
59	Newry	Newry, Church Street	46,50	St.Patricks EC	G
		Downshire Road		2nd P	
		High Street		Convent Chapel	
				Old U	G
		Hill Street		St.Patricks RC Cathedral	
		Kilmorey Street		M	
		Meeting House Lane		RP	G
		Needham Place		St.Marys EC	
				U	
		Postley Place		M	
		Sandys Street		M	
				1st P	
		Trevor Hill		EZ	
		Outley	41		G
		Shannaghan	35	P	
		Sheeptown	46,47	RC	G
		Shinn	41,47	RC	G
60	Newtownards	Ballyblack	6	P	G
		Corporation South	5,6, 11		G
		Milecross	5		G
				Q	
		Movilla	6		G
		Newtownards, Ann Street	5,6	RC	
				COV	
		Church Street		EC	
		Court Street		Ruins	
		Great Francis Street		U	
				P	
		Mark Street		P	
		Regent Street		M	

NGA No.	CIVIL PARISH	TOWNLAND OR TOWN, STREET	OS No.	CHURCH	GRAVE-YARD
60	Newtownards	Newtownards, Regent Street	5,6	P	
				RP	
		South Street		P	
		Zion Place		M	
61	Rathmullan	Killough, Barrack Lane	45	RC	
		Downpatrick Road		M	
		Palatine Square		EC	G
		Rathmullan Upper	44	EC	G
		Rossglass	45	RC	G
62	Saintfield	Bresagh	15,22	P	G
		Saintfield, Cow Market	16	2nd P	G
		Town of Saintfield	16	1st P	G
				EC	G
				RC	
63	Saul	Ballysugagh	31,38	RC	
				RC un-finished	
		Carrowcarlin	31	RC	
		Saul	31,38	EC	G
64	Seapatrick	Banbridge, Church Square	27	2nd U	
		Downshire Road		1st U	
		Dromore Road		RC	
		Gospel Lane		M	
		Main Street			G
		Newry Street		BAP	
		Scarva Street		M	
				P	G
		Killpike	27		G
65	Shankill				
66	Slanes	Slanes	25		G
67	Tullylish	Ballynagarrick Upper	19,26,	P	
		Clare	19,20, 26	RC	
		Coose	26,27	RC	G
		Drumnascamph	26,27	P	G

NGA No.	CIVIL PARISH	TOWNLAND OR TOWN, STREET	OS No.	CHURCH	GRAVE-YARD
67	Tullylish	Gilford, Castle Hill	26	RC	
		Dumbarton Street		M	
				P	
		Moyallen	19,26	M	
		Tullylish	26	EC	G
68	Tullynakill	Tullynakill	11,17	EC	G
69	Tyrella	Tyrella North	44	RC	
					G
		Tyrella South	44	EC	
70	Warrenspoint	Dromore	51,54	M	
		Ringmackilroy	51,54	U	
					G
				P	
					G
		Warrenspoint, Church Street	54	M	
		Great Georges Street		RC	

NGA No.	CIVIL PARISH	TOWNLAND OR TOWN, STREET	OS No.	CHURCH	GRAVE-YARD
1	Aderrig	Aderrig	17		G
2	Artaine	Artaine South	14,15, 18,19		G
3	Baldongan	Baldongan	5,8		G
4	Baldoyle	Town of Baldoyle	15	RC	
		Grange	15		G
5	Balgriffin	St. Doolagh's	15	EC	G
6	Ballyboghill	Ballyboghill	7		G
		Grange	7	RC	
7	Ballyfermot	Ballyfermot Upper	17,18		G
8	Ballymadun	Ballymadun	6	RC	
		Glebe	6		G
9	Balrothery	Balbriggan, Chapel Lane	2,5	Old RC	
		Drogheda Street		M	
		Dublin Street		New RC	G
		George's Street		EC	G
		Village of Balrothery	5	EC	G
				RC	
		Bremore	1,2		G
10	Balscadden	Village of Balscadden	1	RC	
		Tobertown	1,4		G
11	Booterstown	Booterstown, Chapel Court	23	RC	
		Merrion, Cross Avenue		EC	
12	Castleknock	Abbotstown	13,14		G
		Blanchardstown	13,17	RC	
		Cabragh	14,18	RC	
		Castleknock	13,14 17,18	EC	G
13	Chapelizod	Chapelizod	18	RC	
				EC	G
				RC	
				EC	
14	Cloghran	Cloghran	13,14		G
				EC	G

NGA No.	CIVIL PARISH	TOWNLAND OR TOWN, STREET	OS No.	CHURCH	GRAVE-YARD
15	Clondalkin	Clondalkin	17,21	RC	
				EC	
		Knockmitten	17,21	RC	
16	Clonmethan	Glebe	7	EC	G
		Oldtown	7	RC	
17	Clonsilla	Clonsilla	13	EC	G
		Kellystown	13,17	RC	
18	Clontarf	Clontarf East	18,19	EC	G
		Town of Clontarf, Back Lane	19	RC	
19	Clonturk	Ballybough	18		G
				RC	
		Town of Drumcondra	14,18	EC	G
		Richmond	18	RC	
20	Coolock	Brookville	15	RC	
		Tonlegee	15	EC	G
21	Cruagh	Cruagh	25		G
22	Crumlin	Crumlin	18,22	EC	G
				RC	
23	Dalkey	Dalkey	23		G
				RC	
24	Donabate	Donabate	12	EC	G
		Kilcrea	12		G
25	Donnybrook	Donnybrook East, Fair Green	18,20	Convent RC	
		Main Street			G
				RC	
		Irishtown, Irishtown Road	18	EC	G
		Pembroke Street		RC	
		Merrion	18,19, 22,23		G
		Ringsend, Thomas Street	18	M	
		Sandymount, Sandymount Avenue	18,19	Convent RC	
		Smotscourt	18,20	EC	
26	Drimnagh	Bluebell	17,18		G

COUNTY DUBLIN

NGA No.	CIVIL PARISH	TOWNLAND OR TOWN, STREET	OS No.	CHURCH	GRAVE-YARD
27	DUBLIN CITY	See DUBLIN CITY			
28	Esker	Glebe	17		G
29	Finglas	Finglas East	14	EC	
				Old EC	G
				RC	
30	Garristown	Garristown	3,4	EC	G
				RC	
31	Glasnevin	Glasnevin	14,18	EC	G
		Prospect	18	RC	
32	Grallagh	Grallagh	4,7		G
33	Grangegorman	Grangegorman Middle	18	RC	
34	Hollywood	Damastown	4,7	RC	
		Hollywood Great	4		G
35	Holmpatrick	Grange	5		G
		Milvertown	5	RC	
		Skerries, Chapel Street	5	RC	
		Strand Street South		EC	G
36	Howth	Howth	15,16,19	Old Abbey RC	G G
		Howth Demesne	15,16,19	EC	
		Sutton South	15,19		G
37	Kilbarrack	Kilbarrack Low	15		G
38	Kilbride	Kilbride	21		G
39	Kilgobbin	Kilgobbin	22,23,25,26		G
40	Kill	Cabinteely	23,26	RC	
		Kill of the Grange	23		G
41	Killeek	Killeek	11		G
42	Killester	Killester North	14,15,18,19		G
43	Killiney	Killiney	23,26		G
		Loughlinstown	26	EC	G
44	Killossery	Killossery	11		G
		Rowlestown East	7,11	RC	

NGA No.	CIVIL PARISH	TOWNLAND OR TOWN, STREET	OS No.	CHURCH	GRAVE-YARD
45	Kilmactalway	Kilmactalway	21		G
		Loughtown Lower	17,20 21		G
46	Kilmacud				
47	Kilmahuddrick	Kilmahuddrick	17		G
48	Kilsallaghan	Castlefarm	11	EC	G
		Corrstown	11		G
49	Kiltiernan	Glebe	26	EC	
		Glencullen	25,26	RC	G
		Kiltiernan	25,26		G
50	Kinsaley	Kinsaley	12,15		G
				RC	
51	Leixlip				
52	Lucan	Lucan and Pettycanon	17	EC	
				M	
				RC	G
		Lucan Demesne	17		G
53	Lusk	Town of Lusk	8	RC	G
				EC	G
		Town of Rush	8	RC	
		Rush Demesne	8		G
		Whitestown	8		G
54	Malahide	Malahide, The Mall	12	RC	
		Strand Street		EC	G
		Malahide Demesne	12		G
55	Monkstown	Bullock, Harbour Road	23	EC	
		Dunleary, Adelaide Street	23	Mariners Church	
		Longford Terrace		BL	
		Meeting House Road		Q	
		Monkstown Road		EC	
		Northumberland Avenue		M	
				I	
		Sussex Parade		RC	

NGA No.	CIVIL PARISH	TOWNLAND OR TOWN, STREET	OS No.	CHURCH	GRAVE-YARD
55	Monkstown	Dunleary, York Street	23	P	
		Newtown Blackrock, Back Road	23	RC	
		Carysfort Avenue		EC	
		Georges Lane		M	
56	Mulhuddart	Buzzardstown	13		G
57	Naul	Naul	4	EC	G
		Westown	4	RC	
58	Newcastle	Colmanstown	20,21		G
		Glebe	20,21	EC	G
		Newcastle South	20,21	RC	
59	Oldconnaught	Ballyman	26,28		G
		Cork Little	26	EC	
		Little Bray	26	RC	G
		Oldconnaught	26,28		G
60	Palmerstown	Palmerstown	6,7	RC	G
61	Portmarnock	Burrow	15		G
		Portmarnock	15	EC	G
62	Portraine	Beaverstown	8,12	RC	
		Lambay Island	9	RC	G
		Portraine	8		G
64	Raheny	Town of Raheny	15	EC	G
65	Rathcoole	Rathcoole	21	EC	
66	Rathfarnham	Rathfarnham	22	Loretto RC / RC	G
		Town of Rathfarnham	22	EC	
67	Rathmichael	Rathmichael	26		G
68	Saggart	Newtown Upper	21,24		G
		Village of Saggart	21	RC / RC in Progress	

NGA No.	CIVIL PARISH	TOWNLAND OR TOWN, STREET	OS No.	CHURCH	GRAVE- YARD
	St. Catherine's	Mount Jerome	18	Harolds- cross EC	
	St. George's	Clonliff West, Burnett Place	18		G
	St. James's	Goldenbridge North	18	RC M Military Church	G
		Inchicore North	18	P	
69	St. Margaret's	St. Margarets	11,14	RC	G
70	St. Peter's	Baggotrath East, Baggot Street Upper	18	EC	
		Haddington Road		RC	
		Cullenswood, Sandford Terrace	18	EC	
		Haroldscross West	18,22	RC	
		Milltown	18,22	RC EC	
		Ranelagh North,Charlemount Terrace	18	RC	
		Ranelagh South,Cullenswood Avenue	18	M	
		Rathmines East, Carton Terrace	18,22	Convent RC	
		Church Avenue		EC	
		Rathmines Road		RC	
71	Santry	Santry	14	EC	
72	Stillorgan	Stillorgan South	23	EC	G
73	Swords	Balheary	11	RC	
		Swords Demesne	11,12	RC	
		Swords Glebe	11	EC	G
74	Tallaght	Friarstown Upper	21,24 25	RC	
		Glassvullane	24,25, 27		G
		Tallaght	21,22	EC	G
		Templeogue	22		G

NGA No.	CIVIL PARISH	TOWNLAND OR TOWN, STREET	OS No.	CHURCH	GRAVE- YARD
74	Tallaght	Tymon South	22	RC	
75	Taney	Balally	22,25	RC	
		Dundrum, Church Road	22	EC	
		Churchtown Road			G
				RC	
		Farranboley, Milltown	22	RC	
		Roebuck	22	M	
76	Tully	Laughanstown	26		G
77	Ward	Ward Lower	10,11		G
78	Westpalstown	Westpalstown	7		G
79	Whitechurch	Kilmashogue	22,25	EC	
		Whitechurch	22		G
					MO G

NGA No.	CIVIL PARISH	TOWNLAND OR TOWN, STREET	OS No.	CHURCH	GRAVE-YARD
1	Donnybrook				
	Grangegorman	Dalymount	2	RC	
		Phibsborough Road	2,7	EC	
2	Christchurch				
3	St. Andrew's	Eustace Street	21	U	
				Q	
		St. Andrew's Street	21	St. Andrews EC	G
4	St. Anne's	Clarendon Street	21	RC	
		Dawson Street	21,27	St.Annes EC	G
5	St. Audoen's	High Street	20	St. Audoens RC	
				St. Audoens EC	
6	St. Bartholomew's				
7	St. Bridget's	Bride Street	20,26, 27	St. Bridgets EC	G
				Molyneaux Chapel	
		Georges Street Great South	21	M	
		Peter Street	27		French Protes- tant G
		Ship Street Great	21		G
8	St. Catherine's	Brown Street	26	M	
		Cork Street	25,26		Quaker G
				M	
		John's Street West	20	RC	
		Meath Street	29	RC in Progress	
				St. Cather- ines RC	
		Swift's Alley	20	EC	

NGA No.	CIVIL PARISH	TOWNLAND OR TOWN, STREET	OS No.	CHURCH	GRAVE-YARD
8	St. Catherine's	Thomas Street	20	St. Catherines EC	
					G
9	St. George's	Charles Street Great	4,8,9	EC	
		Gardiner Street Upper	8	RC	
		Georges Place North	3,8	St. Georges EC	
		Hardwicke Street	8	M	
		Temple Street Lower	8	EC	G
10	St. James'	Dolphin's Barn	31	RC	
		James' Street	19	St.James RC	
				St.James EC	G
		Military Road			Royal Hospital G
					Bully's Acre G
11	St. John's	Exchange Street Lower	20,21	RC	
		Fishamble Street	20	St.Johns EC	
12	St. Lukes	Coombe	26	St.Lukes EC	
		Mill Street	26	Convent RC	
13	St. Mark's	Brunswick Street Great	21,22	CB	
		College Green	21,22	College Chapel	
		Forbes Street	23	Mariners Chapel	
		Hanover Street East	22	Dutch Chapel	
		Mark Street	22	St.Marks EC	G
		Poolbeg Street	14,15	German Lutheran Church	
		Westland Row	22	St. Andrews RC	

NGA No.	CIVIL PARISH	TOWNLAND OR TOWN, STREET	OS No.	CHURCH	GRAVE-YARD
14	St. Mary's	Capel Street	13,14	P	
		Denmark Street Little	14	RC	
		Dominick Street Lower	8,14	RC Unfinished	
		Dorset Street Upper	8	BA	
		King's Inn Street	8,14	Z	
		Mary's Abbey	13,14	J	
		Mary Street	14	St.Marys EC	G
		Mountjoy Street	7,8	St.Marys EC	
		Strand Street Great	14	U	
15	St. Michael's	High Street	20	St. Michaels EC	
		Merchant's Quay	20	Adam and Eve RC	
16	St. Michan's	Anne Street North	13	RC	
		Church Street	13	RC	
				St. Michans EC	G
		Georges Hill	13	Convent RC	
		King Street North	13	EC	G
		Ormond Quay Upper	14,20 21	P	
17	St. Nicholas' Within	Nicholas Street	20	Site of St. Nicholas EC	Vaults
18	St. Nicholas' Without	Cathedral Lane	26		French G
					Deanery G
		Christchurch Place	20	Christ Church EC	
		Francis Street	20,26	RC	
		Patrick Street	20,26	St. Patricks EC	G
		Plunkett Street	20	I	

DUBLIN CITY

NGA No.	CIVIL PARISH	TOWNLAND OR TOWN, STREET	OS No.	CHURCH	GRAVE-YARD
19	St. Patrick's				
20	St. Paul's	Arbour Hill	12,13	Garrison RC	G
		Arran Quay	13,20	RC	
		Blackhall Place	13	M	
21	St. Peter's	Adelaide Road	32	P	
				St. Matthias EC	
		Aungier Street	21,27	St.Peters EC	G
				M	
				Carmel- ite RC	
		Bishop Street	27	MO	
		Kevin Street Lower (Church Lane)'	27	St. Kevins EC	G
		Leeson Street Lower	27,32 33	Magdal- ene EC	
		Merrion Row	27,28		French G
		Mount Street Crescent	28	St. Stephens EC	
		Stephen's Green South	27	M	
		York Row	27	Carmel- ite RC	
		York Street	27	I	
		Whitefriar Street	21,27	Carmel- ite RC	
22	St. Thomas'	Abbey Street	14	UP	
				M	
				BAP	
		Gardiner Street Lower	8,9, 14,15	Trinity EC	
		Gloucester Street North Lower	8,9	P	

NGA No.	CIVIL PARISH	TOWNLAND OR TOWN, STREET	OS No.	CHURCH	GRAVE-YARD
22	St. Thomas's	Marlborough Street	8,14	St. Thomas' EC	
				RC	
		North Strand	4,5,9	Episc-opal Church	
		Oriel Street Upper	9,15	M	
		Portland Row	9	St. Josephs RC Unfini-shed	
		Seville Place	9	RC	
		Summer Hill	8,9	M	
		Talbot Street	14,15	M	
		William Street North	4	Convent RC	
23	St. Werburgh	Werburgh Street	20	St. Werburghs EC	G

NGA No.	CIVIL PARISH	TOWNLAND OR TOWN, STREET	OS No.	CHURCH	GRAVE-YARD
1	Aghalurcher	Aghalurcher Glebe	34	G	
		Castle Balfour Demesne	34	EC	G
		Cavanaleck	24	P	
		Cooltrane	23,24	EC	G
		Cooneen	24,29	RC	
		Croaghan	34	RC	
		Drumgoon	28	EC	G
		Drummack	28,34	Preaching House	
		Killashanbally	28	P	
		Lisnaskea, Main Street	34	M M	
		Maguiresbridge, Chapel Lane Gledstown Main Street	28	RC M M	G
		Mullaghfad	29,30	EC	
		Tattynuckle	24		G
2	Aghavea	Aghavea	28	EC	G
		Brookeborough, Main Street	28	Preaching House M	
		Lismalore	28	RC	G
		Tattykeeran	23	EC	
3	Belleek	Ballymagaghran	3,4, 8,9	RC	
		Town of Belleek	8	M	
		Leggs	8	EC	
		Rossbeg	8,9		G
		Tievealough	8		G
4	Boho	Carrickbeg	21		G
		Farnaconnell	21	EC	
		Toneel North	20,21	RC	G
5	Clones	Aghadrumsee and Killygorman	35	EC	G
		Cloghmore	36	EC	G
		Drumswords	35	RC	G

NGA No.	CIVIL PARISH	TOWNLAND OR TOWN, STREET	OS No.	CHURCH	GRAVE-YARD
5	Clones	Lisrace	35,40	M	
		Village of Magheraveela	40		G
		Rosslea	36	RC	
6	Cleenish	Bellanaleck	27	EC	G
		Cornagee	26	EC	
		Faughard	27,28	P	G
		Kilrooskagh	25	RC	
		Lisbellaw, Hollybank Road	27	RC	
		Main Street		M	
				EC	G
				M	
		Mullyardlougher	26	RC	
		Mullymesker	26,27	RC	G
		Rushin	25		G
		Templenaffrin	25		G
7	Derrybrusk	Derryharney	27	EC	
8	Derryvullan	Cleenish	27		G
		Coolaness	10	RC	
		Derryvullan	27		G
		Fyagh	27		G
		Irvinestown, Church Street	11	EC	G
		Fair Green		M	
		Pound Street		M	
		Trillick Road			G
		Village of Lisnarick	10		G
		Lissan	22	RC	
		Milltate	11	P	
		Mullies	10	EC	
		Mulrod	27	EC	G
		Tully	15,16	M	
		Whitehill South	16	RC	
9	Devenish	Drumary	14,15	RC	
		Faugher	21	M	
		Monea	15,21	EC	G

NGA No.	CIVIL PARISH	TOWNLAND OR TOWN, STREET	OS No.	CHURCH	GRAVE-YARD
9	Devenish	Village of Monea	15	RC	
10	Drumkeeran	Bannagh More	5	RC	
		Keeran	6	EC	
		Killynoogan	4,5	M	
		Monavreece	6	RC	
		Montiaghroe	1	RC	
		Town of Pettigoe	4	P	
				M	
		Tubbrid	5	EC	G
11	Drummully	Cloncallick	43	P	G
		Drummully	43		G
12	Enniskillen	Camgart	17,18	Site for new EC	
		Cornagrade	22		G
		Enniskillen, Belmore Street	22	Convent Chapel	G
		Bridge Street East		M	
				P	
		Church Street		EC	G
		Darling Street		RC	
		Wesley Street		M	
		Inishkeen	27		G
		Pubble	23	M	
					G
		Town of Tempo	23	EC	G
				P	G
				RC	
				M	
13	Galloon	Donagh	34,39		G
		Drumquillia	40	RC	
		Galloon	42		G
		Moorlough	34	RC	
		Newtownbutler, Clones Street	40	M	
		Main Street		EC	G

NGA No.	CIVIL PARISH	TOWNLAND OR TOWN, STREET	OS No.	CHURCH	GRAVE-YARD
13	Galloon	Newtownbutler, Main Street	40	M	
		Sallaghy	34,39	EC	
14	Inishmacsaint	Aghamore	14		G
		Binmore Glebe	10	EC	G
		Carrigolagh	8	EC	
		Village of Church Hill	9	M	
		Cosbystown	15	M	
		Derrygonnelly, Fair Green	15	M	
		Knockarevan	13	RC	G
				EC	G
		Rosscor	8	RC	
		Slawin	8		G
15	Killesher	Derrylester	32	RC	
		Drumduff	32	M	
		Druminiskill	27,32 33	EC	
		Drumlaghy	32	M	
		Killesher	26,32		G
		Knockageehan	26,32	M	
		Mullynahunshin	32	RC	
		Tullyhona	32	EC	
16	Kinawley	Callowhill	38		G
		Cloghan	38	EC	
		Derrylin	38	RC	
		Derryvore	39,42	EC	
		Drumderg	41	RC	
		Glasmullagh	42	RC	
		Lismonaghan	33	RC	G
17	Magheracross	Village of Bellanamallard	16	EC	G
				M	
				M	
		Coa	16	RC	
		Knockmanoul	16	M	
				M	
		Magheracross	16		G

NGA No.	CIVIL PARISH	TOWNLAND OR TOWN, STREET	OS No.	CHURCH	GRAVE-YARD
18	Magheraculmoney	Ederny, Main Street	6	Upper Storey of Market House used for Religious Services	
		Tullanaglug	5,6	EC	G
19	Rossorry	Mullaghy	26,27	M	
		Mullanacaw	22	EC	G
		Rossorry	22		G
20	Templecarn				
21	Tomregan				
22	Trory	Laragh	16	M	
		Trory	16	EC	G

NGA No.	CIVIL PARISH	TOWNLAND OR TOWN, STREET	OS No.	CHURCH	GRAVE-YARD
1	Abbeygormacan	Mullaghmore	98,99 106,107	RC	
2	Abbeyknockmoy	Chapelfield	58	RC	
3	Addergoole	Carrowntomush	4,16		G
4	Ahascragh	Ahascragh, Main Street	61,74		G
		Ahascragh West	61,74	EC RC	G
		Lattoon	60,61		G
5	Annaghdown	Annaghdown	56,69		G
		Aucloggeen	56,57, 69,70	EC	G
		Carrowbeg South	56,69	RC	
6	Ardrahan	Ardrahan North	114	EC	
		Ballylara	113,114	RC	
		Castledaly	114	RC	
		Lydacan	113		G
7	Athenry	Athenry	84	EC	G
		Ballydavid North	71,84		G
		Carnaun	84		G
		Cullairbaun	84	RC	
8	Athleague	Coolaspaddaun	20,33		G
		Monasternalea or Abbeygrey	33		G
9	Aughrim	Town of Aughrim	87	M RC	
		Foats or Levallynearl	87	EC	G
10	Ballindoon	Callow	49,50, 62		G
		Derrigimlagh	35,49	RC	
		Drinagh	35	EC	
11	Ballymacward	Alloon Upper	60,73	RC	
		Ballymacward	73	EC	G
12	Ballynacourty	Ballynacourty	95,103		G
		Kilcaimin	95		G
		Knockawuddy	95,103	RC	

NGA No.	CIVIL PARISH	TOWNLAND OR TOWN, STREET	OS No.	CHURCH	GRAVE-YARD
13	Ballynakill	Ballynakill	7		G
		Ballynakill	116		G
		Cuilleendaeagh	125		G
		Curragh	116		G
		Derryherbert	10	RC	
		Foher	10,11	EC	
		Friary	125		G
		Garraunbaun	22	RC	
		Garrynaglogh	116,125 126	RC	
		Keelogesbeg	7	RC	
		Knockadrum	125	RC	
		Lecknavarna	10,11	RC	
		Letterfrack	26	Meeting House	
		Looscaun	132	RC	
		Moyard	22,23	EC	
		Moyglass	125		Childrens G
		Rosmore	126,132		G
		Woodford	125,131	RC	
		Woodford Main Street	125,131	EC	G
14	Beagh	Ardamullivan	128,129		G
		Ashfield Demesne	128	RC	
		Beagh	123,129		G
15	Belclare	Claretuam	43		G
		Pollaturk or Newgarden	43	RC	G
16	Boyounagh	Cashel	6,18		G
		Glenamaddy	18	RC	G
17	Bullaun	Bullaun	97	RC	G
18	Cargin				
19	Claregalway	Claregalway	69,70	RC	G
		Kiltroge	70		G

NGA No.	CIVIL PARISH	TOWNLAND OR TOWN, STREET	OS No.	CHURCH	GRAVE-YARD
19	Claregalway	Lakeview	53,70	RC	
20	Clonbern	Lerhin	18,31	RC	
		Mahanagh	30,31	RC	
21	Clonfert	Ballynakill	108,109		G
		Coolacurn South	100,101	RC	
		Glebe	101	EC	G
		Town of Laurencetown	100	RC	
				EC	
22	Clonkeen	Ballyglass	72	RC	
		Clonkeenkerrill	59,72		G
	Clonrush	Gweeneeny	135	RC	
23	Clontuskert	Crossconnellmore	99	RC	
		Glenloughaun	87	EC	
		Templepark	87		G
24	Cong				
25	Cummer	Ballybanagher	57	RC	
		Currylaur	57	RC	
		Glebe	43		G
26	Donaghpatrick	Abbeytown	42		G
		Carheenard	42	RC	
		Donaghpatrick	42		G
27	Donanaghta	Eyrecourt Demesne	100	EC	
			108		G
		Eyrecourt, Main Street	108	RC	
		Market Street		M	
		Market Street		EC	
28	Drumacoo	Ballinderreen	103	RC	
		Drumacoo	103		G
29	Drumatemple	Durrow	2	RC	
				EC	
	Dunamon	Dunamon	8		G
				EC	
30	Duniry	Cartron	116	RC	
		Clonlee	116	RC	

NGA No.	CIVIL PARISH	TOWNLAND OR TOWN, STREET	OS No.	CHURCH	GRAVE-YARD
31	Dunmore	Town of Dunmore	17	RC	G
				EC	
		Garrafrauns	4,5,16	RC	
		Newton (Lynott)	30	RC	G
32	Fahy				
33	Fohanagh	Ballydoogan	73	RC	
34	Grange				
35	Inishbofin				
	Inishcaltra	Cappaduff	134,136	RC	
		Inishcaltra or Holy Island	134		G
		Village of Mountshannon	134,136	EC	G
36	Inisheer	Inisheer	119,120	RC	
37	Inishmaan	Carrowntemple	119	RC	
38	Inishmore	Village of Kilronan	110,111 119	EC	
		Oghil	110,111	RC	
39	Isertkelly				
	Kilbarron	Illaunmore	135		G
40	Kilbeacanty	Kilbeacanty	123	RC	
					G
		Streamstown	123		G
41	Kilbegnet	Garraun North	19,20	RC	
		Kilbegnet	7,19,20		G
42	Kilbennan	Pollacorragune	29		G
		Tonlegee	29	RC	
43	Kilchreest	Ballingarry	105	RC	
		Kilchreest, Main Street	105		G
44	Kilcloony	Ballinasloe, Church Hill	53,87,88	EC	
		Church Lane		M	
		Market Square		EC in Progress	
		Society Street		P	
		Tea Lane		Temporary RC Chapel	

NGA No.	CIVIL PARISH	TOWNLAND OR TOWN, STREET	OS No.	CHURCH	GRAVE-YARD
44	Kilcloony	Garbally Demesne	87		G
		Kilcloony	74,87		G
45	Kilcolgan	Kilcolgan	103		G
				EC	
46	Kilconickny	Conicar	105	RC	
		Tooloobauntemple	97		G
47	Kilconierin	Kilconierin	96	RC	G
48	Kilconla	Ballynagittagh	15,28	RC	
		Blindwell	15	EC	G
49	Kilconnell	Glebe	86	EC	
					G
		Village of Kilconnell	73,86 87	RC	
50	Kilcooly				
51	Kilcoona				
52	Kilcroan				
53	Kilcummin	Canrawer East	54	RC	
		Canrawer West	54		G
		Garrynagry	68	RC	
		Gortnashingaun	39,40	RC	
		Lemonfield	54		G
		Lettermullan (Island)	89	RC	
		Oughterard, Main Street	54	EC	G
		Rosmuck	65,78	RC	
54	Kilgerrill	Caltraghlea	74	RC	G
		Kilgerrill	74		G
55	Kilkerrin	Carrowleana	31	RC	
		Glebe	31	EC	G
		Kilkerrin	31		G
56	Kilkilvery	Bunanraun	42	RC	
		Deerpark	42	EC	G
57	Killaan	Ashbrook	86		G
		Killaan	86		G
		Knockbrack	86	RC	

COUNTY GALWAY

NGA No.	CIVIL PARISH	TOWNLAND OR TOWN, STREET	OS No.	CHURCH	GRAVE-YARD
58	Killallaghtan	Cappataggle	86,98	RC	
		Killallaghtan	99		G
59	Killannin	Aille	92	RC	
		Village of Ballynahowna	92	EC	
		Barraderry	90	RC	
		Inveran	91	RC	
		Killannin	68		G
		Maumeen - Knock	78,89 90		G
		Village of Trabane	90	RC	
60	Killeany	Cloghanower	42	EC	G
61	Killeely	Carrigeen East	96,104		G
		Killeelymore	103		G
		Roevehagh	95,103	RC	
62	Killeenadeema	Derrybrien East	124,130		G
		Derrybrien West	124	RC	
		Killeenadeema West	105,115	RC	G
63	Killeenavarra	Ballyclery	113		G
		Killeenavarra	113		G
		Killeeneenmore	95,96 103,104		G
64	Killeenen				
65	Killererin	Carrowmanagh	44	RC	
		Lissavally	44	EC	G
66	Killeroran	Ballygar, Main Street	33	EC	
		Killeroran	33,47		G
67	Killian	Cloonascarberry (Cheevers)	32,46	RC	
		Tohergar	47	RC	
68	Killimorbologue	Boley	118	RC Dominican Convent	
		Garryad and Garryduff	117	RC	
		Killimor and Boleybeg	107		G
69	Killimordaly	Killimor	85	RC	G
70	Killinan	Castleboy	114	EC	G
71	Killinny	Killinny East	122		G

104

NGA No.	CIVIL PARISH	TOWNLAND OR TOWN, STREET	OS No.	CHURCH	GRAVE-YARD
72	Killogilleen	Ballymanagh	104	RC	
73	Killora	Craughwell	90	RC	
		Killora	96,104		G
74	Killoran	Killoran	99	RC	
75	Killoscobe	Killoscobe	59		G
		Menlough Commons	59	RC	
76	Killosolan	Caltra	46,60	RC	
		Castleblakeney	60	EC	G
77	Killower	Ballintleva	42	RC	
78	Killursa	Clerhaun	41	RC	
		Ower	41		G
		Ross	41		G
79	Kilmacduagh	Cloonteen	122	RC	
		Gort, Church Street	122	RC	
		Queen Street		EC	G
		Lisnagyreeny	122		G
80	Kilmalinoge				
81	Kilmeen	Ballydoogan	106	RC	
		Kilmeen	106		G
82	Kilmoylan	Annagh	57,58		G
		Ballyglooneen	57,58	RC	
83	Kilquain	Killachunna	107,108	RC	
84	Kilreekil	Kilboght	98		G
		Wallscourt	98	RC	G
85	Kiltartan	Kiltartan	122,123	RC	
					G
		Lavally	123		G
86	Kilteskil	Ballyeighter	115	RC	
87	Kilthomas	Carrowbaun	97	RC	
		Dromorehill	114,123		G
		Garden Blake	114,123	RC	
					G
88	Kiltormer	Kiltormer, the Abbey Road and Fair Green	99	RC	

NGA No.	CIVIL PARISH	TOWNLAND OR TOWN, STREET	OS No.	CHURCH	GRAVE-YARD
88	Kiltormer	Kiltormer West	99		G
		Newtowneyre	99	EC	G
89	Kiltullagh	Clogharevaun	85,97	RC	
		Esker	84,96	RC	
		Kiltullagh North	85,97		G
90	Kinvarradoorus	Ballybranagan	113	RC	
		Doorus	102,112		G
		Kinvarra, Main Street	113		G
		New Street		EC	
		Newtownlynch	102,112	RC	
91	Lackagh	Lackagh	70	RC	
92	Leitrim	Carrowkeel	106	RC	
		Leitrim More	116		G
93	Lickerrig	Bookeen South	97	EC	
94	Lickmolassy	Gortnacooheen	117	RC	
		Portumna	126,127		G
		Portumna, Boherboy	126,127	RC	G
		Portumna Demesne	126,127	EC	G
95	Liskeevy	Banagher	16	RC	
96	Loughrea	Cosmona	105	RC	
		Loughrea, Abbey Lane	105	RC	G
		Bride Street		RC	
		Church Lane		EC	G
		The Hill			St. Bridget's G
		St. Laurencesfield	105		G
97	Meelick	Carrownafinnoge	108	RC	
		Friarsland	108,109	RC	G
98	Monivea	Caherlissakill	71	RC	
		Town of Monivea	71	EC	G
		Shoodaun	71,72, 84,85	RC	
99	Moycullen	Ballycuirke West	68,81	RC	G
		Killagoola	81		G

NGA No.	CIVIL PARISH	TOWNLAND OR TOWN, STREET	OS No.	CHURCH	GRAVE-YARD
99	Moycullen	Moycullen	68,81		G
		Village of Spiddle	92	RC	
					G
100	Moylough	Mountbellew Demesne	45,46	RC	
		Moyloughmore	45	EC	G
		Village of Newtown Bellew	45	RC	
		Skehanagh	59	RC	
		Treanrevagh	46	Monastery Chapel	
101	Moyrus	Ardbear	35		G
		Ballinafad	37,51	RC	G
		Carna	64,76,77	RC	
		Ervallagh	63	Monastery Chapel	
		Town of Roundstone	50,63	RC	G
				EC	G
					G
				P	G
102	Omey	Claddaghduff	21,22	RC	
		Clifden, Chapel Lane	35	RC	G
		Church Street		EC	G
		Emlagh	21,22	EC	G
		Tullyvoheen	35		G
103	Oranmore	Oranmore, Main Street	95	RC	G
				EC	G
104	Rahoon	Ballagh	81,82	RC	
		Galway, Claddagh	94	RC	G
		Presentation Street		RC	
		Knockaunnacarragh	93	RC	
		Rahoon	81,82,84		G
		Seapoint	93		G
		Tievegarriff	94	RC	
105	Ross	Cloonbur	27	EC	
				RC	

NGA No.	CIVIL PARISH	TOWNLAND OR TOWN, STREET	OS No.	CHURCH	GRAVE-YARD
105	Ross	Kilmeelickin	25	RC	
106	St. Nicholas	Castlegar	82	RC	
		Galway, College Road	82,94	St. Patricks RC	
		Forthill Road		RC	G
		Lombard Street		St. Nicholas EC	G
		Lower Abbey Gate Street		St. Nicholas RC	
		Middle Street		August-inian RC	
		Nuns Island	94	Francis-can RC	
				P	
		St. Francis Street	82,94	RC	G
		St. Vincents Ave.		St. Vincents RC	
		Victoria Place		M	
107	Stradbally	Stradbally North	103	RC	
				Abbey Chapel	
		Stradbally South	103		G
108	Taghboy				
109	Templetogher	Corralough	6	RC	
		Kildaree	6		G
		Straid	6		G
110	Tiranscraght	Longford	108,118	RC	
111	Tuam	Ballymoat	29,43, 44		G
		Cartron	30	RC	
		Tuam, Bishop Street	29	RC	
		Church Lane	29,43	Church in ruins	G
				EC	G
		Townparks (3rd. Division)	29	RC	

NGA No.	CIVIL PARISH	TOWNLAND OR TOWN, STREET	OS No.	CHURCH	GRAVE-YARD
111	Tuam	Townparks (3rd. Division)	29	Sisters of Charitys RC	
112	Tynagh	Killeen South	126	RC	
		Lissanard West	117	RC	
		Tynagh	117	EC	G

COUNTY KERRY

NGA No.	CIVIL PARISH	TOWNLAND OR TOWN, STREET	OS No.	CHURCH	GRAVE-YARD
1	Aghadoe	Coolgarriv	58,66		G
		Fossa	66	RC	
		Knoppoge	58,66	EC	G
		Parkavonear	58,66		G
		Shronedarragh	67,68	RC	
2	Aghavallen	Astee West	2	RC	
		Town of Ballylongford	2,5	RC	
		Lislaughtin	2,3, 6		G
		Rusheen	2,3	EC	G
3	Aglish	Aglish	58	EC	G
4	Annagh	Annagh	37,38		G
		Village of Blennerville Main Street	29,38	EC	G
		Curraheen	37	RC	
5	Ardfert	Town of Ardfert	20,21	EC RC	G
6	Ballincuslane	Cordal East	40,41 49	RC	G
		Cordal West	40	EC	
		Kilquane	40,41		G
7	Ballinvoher	Fahan	52		G
		Inch East	45		G
		Lack	45,46	RC	
8	Ballyconry				
9	Ballyduff	Village of Anascaul	44,45 54,55	RC EC	G
		Ballyduff	35,44		G
10	Ballyheige	Ballyheige	14	EC	G
		Booleenshare	14	RC	
		Glenderry	13,14		G
11	Ballymacelligott	Ballydwyer East	30,39	RC	
		Ballymacelligott	39	EC	G
		Cloghermore	30,39	M	

NGA No.	CIVIL PARISH	TOWNLAND OR TOWN, STREET	OS No.	CHURCH	GRAVE-YARD
11	Ballymacelligott	Coolnadead	39	RC	
12	Ballynacourty	Ballynacourty	44		G
		Brackloon	44,45, 55	RC	
13	Ballynahaglish	Village of Chapeltown	28	RC	
		Glebe	28	EC	G
14	Ballyseedy	Ballyseedy	29,38		G
		Lissardboola	38	EC	
15	Brosna	Village of Brosna	24,32	RC	
		Kilmaniheen West	23,24	EC	
16	Caher	Cahersiveen	79	RC	
				EC	G
		Cloghanelvinaghan	69,79		G
17	Castleisland	Castleisland, Chapel Street	39,40	RC	
		Church Lane		EC	G
		Kilbannivane	40		G
		Knocknagashel West	23	RC	
		Meenbannivane	23,31		G
		Village of Scartaglin	49	RC	
18	Cloghane	Cloghane	34,35	RC	
				EC	G
19	Clogherbrien	Clogherbrien	29		G
20	Currans	Ardcrone	48		G
		Meanus	39,48	RC	
21	Dingle	Ballymorereagh	42,43		G
		Commons of Dingle	43		G
		Dingle, Green Lane	43	RC	
				Nunnery Chapel	
		Main Street		EC	G
		Killelane	43		G
		Milltown	43,53		G
		Raheenyhooig	53		G
22	Dromod	Mastergeehy	89	RC	
		Sallahig	89		G

NGA No.	CIVIL PARISH	TOWNLAND OR TOWN, STREET	OS No.	CHURCH	GRAVE-YARD
23	Duagh	Village of Duagh	17	RC EC	
		Islandboy	11,17		G
24	Dunquin	Ballintemple	42,52		G
		Great Blasket Island	57,61		G
		Inishtooskert Island	51		G
25	Dunurlin	Gortadoo	42		G
		Gortmore	42	RC EC	
		Inishvickillane (Island No 78)	61		G
26	Dysert	Dysert	10		G
		Farran	39		G
		Kilsarkan East	49,59		G
27	Fenit				
28	Finuge				
29	Galey	Ballydonohoe	5,10	RC	
		Garryard	10		G
30	Garfinny	Garfinny	43,53		G
31	Glanbehy	Ballynakilly Lower	63,71		G
		Gowlane	63	RC	
		Kilnabrack Upper	63	EC	
32	Kenmare	Kenmare Old	93		G
		Kenmare, Shelbourne Street and Sound Road	93	RC M	
		Killowen	93	EC	
33	Kilbonane	Kilbonane	57,65		G
		Listry	57	RC	
34	Kilcaragh	Monument	16	RC	
35	Kilcaskan	Garranes	102		G
		Milleens	102	RC	
36	Kilcolman	Farranmanagh	57		G
		Kilcolman	47,57		G
		Milltown, Chapel Square	47	RC	

NGA No.	CIVIL PARISH	TOWNLAND OR TOWN, STREET	OS No.	CHURCH	GRAVE-YARD
36	Kilcolman	Milltown, Church Street	47	Monastery Convent Chapel M P EC	G
37	Kilconly	KIlconly North	1		G
38	Kilcredane	Ballyhar	58	RC	
39	Kilcrohane	Ballycarnahan	106	RC	
		Behaghane	106,107	RC	G
		Darrynane More	106	RC	
		Village of Sneem	99,100	RC	
				EC	G
		Tahilla	100	RC	
		Toor	98,106	RC	
40	Kilcummin	Clashnagarrane	58,59	RC	
		Coom	60	RC Part of	
		Freemount	60,68		G
		Glebe	58		G
		Gneevgullia	60	RC	
		Gortanahaneboy East	68	RC	
41	Kildrum	Ballyeightragh	42,43		G
		Cloghane	52	EC RC	
42	Kilfeighny	Irramore	16	RC	
		Kilfeighny North	16		G
43	Kilflyn	Ballyconnell	21	EC	G
		Castletown	21,22	RC	
44	Kilgarrylander	Boolteens West	37,38, 46,47	RC	
		Keel	46		G
45	Kilgarvan	Village of Kilgarvan	85,94	RC	G
46	Kilgobban	Ballinknockane	37,56	RC	
47	Killaha	Killaha	67,75		G
48	Killahan	Tonaknock	15,21		G
49	Killarney	Inch	66	RC	
				RC Cathedral in progress	

NGA No.	CIVIL PARISH	TOWNLAND OR TOWN, STREET	OS No.	CHURCH	GRAVE-YARD
49	Killarney	Killarney, High Street	66	M	
				Convent	
		Main Street		EC	G
		Upper New Street		RC	
		Killegy Lower	66,67, 74,75		G
		Muckross	66,74		G
50	Killeentierna	Killeentierna	48,49	EC	G
		Ranalough	48	RC	
51	Killehenny	Ballyeagh	4,9		G
		Doon West	4	RC	
		Killehenny	4		G
52	Killemlagh	Doory	87	RC	
		Rathkieran	89,96		G
53	Killinane	Ballynahow More	70	RC	
		Glebe	80		G
		Kells	62,70		G
54	Killiney	Killiney	35,36	EC	G
		Kilshannig	19,27		G
		Martramane	27,36	RC	
55	Killorglin	Dromavally	56		G
		Kilcoolaght East	65		G
		Killorglin, Main Street	56	EC	
		Mill Road		RC	
56	Killury	Dromkeen West	15	RC	
		Lissycurrig	14,15	EC	G
57	Kilmalkedar	Carrig	33,42	RC	
		Gallarus	42		G
		Kilmalkedar	42,43		G
58	Kilmoyly	Kilmoyly South	14,15 20,21		G
		Lerrig South	20,21	RC	
59	Kilnanare	Kilnanare	47		G
60	Kilnaughtin	Carhoona	3		G

NGA No.	CIVIL PARISH	TOWNLAND OR TOWN, STREET	OS No.	CHURCH	GRAVE-YARD
60	Kilnaughtin	Tarbert, Chapel Street	3	RC	
		Church Street		M	
		Tieraclea Lower	3	EC	
61	Kilquane	Kilquane	34		G
62	Kilshenane	Gortacloghane	17,23		G
		Kilshenane	16		G
63	Kiltallagh	Cloghleagh	47	RC	
		Gransha Lower	47	EC	G
64	Kiltomy	Kiltomy	15		G
65	Kinard	Kinard East	53,54		G
66	Knocknane	Churchtown	65	EC	
		Cloon West	81,82, 90.91		G
		Coolmagort	65	RC	
		Kilgobnet	65		G
		Moyleglass	72,82		G
		Shanacashel	72	RC	
		Shronahiree More	72,82		G
67	Knockanure	Kealid	11	RC	
		Lissaniska	11		G
68	Lisselton	Loughanes	10	EC	G
69	Listowel	Curraghatoosane	10		G
				RC	
		Listowel, The Square	10,11	RC	
				EC	
70	Marhin	Ballineanig Churchquarter	42		G
71	Minard	Aglish	54		G
		Graigue	44,54	RC	
72	Molahiffe	Castlefarm	48		G
		Corbally	48	RC	
		Roxborough	48	EC	
73	Murher	Murher	6,11		G
		Village of Newtown Sandes	6,11	RC	

COUNTY KERRY

NGA No.	CIVIL PARISH	TOWNLAND OR TOWN, STREET	OS No.	CHURCH	GRAVE-YARD
74	Nohaval	Ballyegan	30,39		G
75	Nohavaldaly				
76	O'Brennan	Crag	30		G
77	O'Dorney	Village of Abbeydorney	21	RC	
		Knockaunmore	21		G
78	Prior	Ballinskelligs	97		G
		Dungeagan	97	RC	
		Emlaghdreen	88,97	EC	
79	Ratass	Ratass	29		G
80	Rattoo	Village of Ballyduff	9	RC	
		Derryco	9		G
		Knockananore	9		G
		Rattoo	9		G
81	Stradbally				
82	Templenoe	Dromore	92,101	EC	
		Greenane	98		G
		Rossacoosane	92	RC	
83	Tralee	Cloonalour, Listowel New Road	29	P	
		Tralee, Brewery Road	29		G
		Castle Street Lower	29	EC	G
				RC	
				Presentation Convent	
		Denny Street		M	
		Nelson Street		EC	G
		Princes Quay		I	
84	Tuosist	Dawros	92,101 102	RC	
		Derreen	108,109	RC	
		Kilmakilloge	108		G
85	Valencia	Ballyhearny West	78,79 87,88	RC	
		Farranreagh	79	EC	G
					G

NGA No.	CIVIL PARISH	TOWNLAND OR TOWN, STREET	OS No.	CHURCH	GRAVE- YARD
86	Ventry	Cantra	52	RC	
		Kilfarnoge	52		G
		Ventry	52		G

NGA No.	CIVIL PARISH	TOWNLAND OR TOWN, STREET	OS No.	CHURCH	GRAVE- YARD
1	Ardkill	Ballyshannon	8		G
		Derrinturn	8	RC	
2	Ardree	Ardree	35		G
3	Ballaghmoon	Ballaghmoon	39		G
	Ballybought	Ballybought	29		G
4	Ballybrackan	Fasagh	26		G
		Lughil	26		G
5	Ballymany				
6	Ballymore Eustace	Ballymore Eustace East	25,29	EC	G
		Town of Ballymore Eustace	25,29	RC	
7	Ballynadrumny	Garrisker	3	RC	
8	Ballynafagh	Ballynafagh	13	EC	G
		Staplestown	9	RC	
9	Ballysax	Ballysax Great	28	EC	G
10	Ballyshannon	Ballyshannon Demesne	28,32	EC	G
11	Balraheen	Barreen	10		G
		Rathcoffey North	10	RC	
12	Belan	Belan	38		G
13	Bodenstown				
14	Brannockstown				
15	Brideschurch	Waterstown	19		G
16	Cadamstown	Cadamstown	3		G
		Town of Johnstown	4	RC	
17	Carbury	Carbury	8		G
				EC	
					G
18	Carn	Churchland East	28		G
		Common South	28	RC	G
19	Carnalway	Carnalway	29	EC	
20	Carragh	Carragh	18,19		G
				RC	
		Donore	13,18	EC	
21	Carrick				
22	Castledermot	Town of Castledermot	38,40	RC	

NGA No.	CIVIL PARISH	TOWNLAND OR TOWN, STREET	OS No.	CHURCH	GRAVE-YARD
22	Castledermot	Town of Castledermot		EC	G
		Hobartstown West	38		G
23	Castledillon	Castledillon Upper	14,15		G
24	Churchtown	Raheenadeeragh	34		G
		Woodstock North	35		G
25	Clane	Abbeyland	14		G
		Town of Clane	14	EC	G
				RC	
26	Clonaghlis	Clonaghlis	15		G
27	Cloncurry	Cloncurry	4		G
		Killeighter	4		G
		Newtown	4	RC	G
28	Clonshanbo	Clonshanbo	9,10		G
	Coghlanstown	Coghlanstown	29		G
29	Confey	Confey	6,11		G
30	Davidstown	Colbinstown	32,36		G
		Davidstown	32		G
31	Donadea	Donadea South	9	EC	G
32	Donaghcumper	Donaghcumper	11		G
33	Donaghmore	Donaghmore	6		G
34	Downings	Downings North	13		G
35	Duneany	Duneany	27		G
36	Dunfierth	Kilshanchoe	3	RC	
37	Dunmanoge	Dunmanoge	39		G
		Maganey Upper	37,39	RC	G
38	Dunmurraghill				
39	Dunmurry	Dunmurry East	22		G
40	Feighcullen	Feighcullen	17	EC	G
		Milltown	18,23	RC	G
41	Fontstown	Fontstown Lower	31		G
				EC	
		Tippeenan Lower	31		G
42	Forenaghts				
43	Gilltown	Gilltown	29		G

COUNTY KILDARE

NGA No.	CIVIL PARISH	TOWNLAND OR TOWN, STREET	OS No.	CHURCH	GRAVE-YARD
44	Graney	Knockpatrick	38,40		G
45	Grangeclare				
46	Grangerosnolvan				
47	Greatconnell	Blackrath and Athgarvan	23		G
		Greatconnell	23		G
				EC	G
48	Harristown	Harristown Lower	27		G
49	Haynestown				
	Jago	Gaganstown	29		G
50	Johnstown	Village of Johnstown	19		G
51	Kerdiffstown				
52	Kilberry	Cloney	30,31		G
		Geraldine	35		G
		Kilberry	30,31		G
				EC	G
		Tyrrellstown	35		G
53	Kilcock	Kilcock, Chapel Lane	5	RC	
		Church Lane		EC	G
54	Kilcullen	Castlemartin	28		G
		Gormanstown	28,29	RC	
					G
		Nicholastown	28	RC	G
		Oldkilcullen	28		G
		Yellowbogcommon	28	EC	G
55	Kildangan	Kildangan			G
				RC	
56	Kildare	Kildare	22		G
		Kildare, Chapel Street	22	RC	G
		Church and Friary Lane		St Brigids EC	G
		Rathangan Road		Friary RC	G
57	Kildrought	Celbridge, Church Street	11	EC	
		Main Street		M	

NGA No.	CIVIL PARISH	TOWNLAND OR TOWN, STREET	OS No.	CHURCH	GRAVE-YARD
57	Kildrought	Celbridge, Main Street		RC	
		Oakley Park	11		G
58	Kilkea	Kilkea Lower	37,38		G
59	Kill	Town of Kill	14,19, 20	RC	
				EC	G
60	Killadoon	Killadoon	11		G
61	Killashee	Killashee	24	EC	
		Stephenstown North	24	RC	G
62	Killelan	Killelan	38		G
63	Killybegs	Town of Prosperous	13	RC	
64	Kilmacredock				
65	Kilmeage	Ballintine	17,18		G
					G
		Town of Kilmeage	18	EC	
66	Kilmore				
67	Kilpatrick	Kilpatrick	12		G
68	Kilrainy	Kilrainy	2,3,		G
69	Kilrush	Castlefarm	32		G
70	Kilteel				
71	Kineagh				
72	Knavinstown	Knavinstown	22		G
73	Lackagh	Clogheen	21		G
		Lackaghmore	22	EC	G
74	Ladytown	Ladytown	18,19, 23,24		G
75	Laraghbryan	Laraghbryan East	5		G
		Mariavilla	5	RC	
		Maynooth, Nunnery Lane	5	RC	
		Parson's Street		EC	
		Oldcarton	6		G
76	Leixlip	Leixlip	6,11	RC	
		Leixlip, Main Street	6,11	EC	G
77	Lullymore	Lullymore East	12		G
78	Lyons	Ardclogh	14,15	RC	

COUNTY KILDARE

NGA No.	CIVIL PARISH	TOWNLAND OR TOWN, STREET	OS No.	CHURCH	GRAVE-YARD
78	Lyons	Lyons	15		G
79	Mainham	Castlebrown or Clongowes	10,14	College RC	
		Mainham	10,14		G
80	Monasterevin	Monasterevin, Drogheda Street	24,26	RC	
		Main Street	24,26	EC	G
				M	
		Passlands	21	RC	G
81	Moone	Ardscull	31,35		G
		Burtown Big	35,36		G
		Moone	36,38	RC	G
					G
82	Morristownbiller	Common	23	Friary RC	
		Moorfield	23	EC	G
		Morristownbiller	23		G
83	Mylerstown				
84	Naas	Maudlings	19		G
		Naas, Back Lane	19		G
		Main Street		EC	G
		Sallins Road		Convent RC	
				RC	
85	Narraghmore	Blackrath	32		G
		Crookstown Upper	36	RC	
		Glassely	32,33		G
		Kilmead	31,35	RC	
		Moyleabbey	36	RC	
					G
		Narraghmore Demesne	32	EC	G
86	Nurney	Killinagh	2,3	RC	
		Nurney	3		G
		Nurney	27,31	RC	G
		Nurney Demesne	27	EC	
87	Oldconnell	Barrettstown	18		G

NGA No.	CIVIL PARISH	TOWNLAND OR TOWN, STREET	OS No.	CHURCH	GRAVE-YARD
87	Oldconnell	Oldconnell	18,23		G
				RC	
				RC	
88	Oughterard				
89	Painestown				
90	Pollardstown	Pollardstown	23		G
91	Rathangan	Rathangan, Main Street	17	RC	
				EC	
92	Rathernan	Grangehiggin	18	RC	G
		Rathernan	18		G
93	Rathmore	Blackhall	24		G
		Crosscoolharbour	25	RC	
		Rathmore West	19,20, 25	EC	G
				RC	
94	St John's	Athy, Saint John's Lane	35		G
95	St Michael's	Athy	35		G
		Athy, Meeting House Lane	35	M	
		Ophally Street		EC	
		Stanhope Street		RC	
96	Scullogestown	Hortland	4,9		G
97	Sherlockstown				
98	Stacummy				
99	Straffan	Straffan	10,14	RC	
				EC	G
100	Taghadoe	Cowanstown	10		G
		Taghadoe	10	EC	G
101	Tankardstown	Nicholastown	37		G
		Rosetown	37		G
102	Thomastown	Thomastown East	17,22	EC	G
103	Timahoe	Hodgestown	9		Quaker G
		Timahoe East	9		G
104	Timolin	Ballitore	36		Quaker G
		Town of Ballitore	36	Q	

NGA No.	CIVIL PARISH	TOWNLAND OR TOWN, STREET	OS No.	CHURCH	GRAVE-YARD
104	Timolin	Village of Timolin	36	EC	G
105	Tipper				
106	Tipperkevin	Commons	24		G
		Glebe West	24	EC	
107	Tully	Moortown	28		G
		Rathbride	22,23		G
108	Usk				
109	Walterstown				
110	Whitechurch	Whitechurch	14		G

COUNTY KILKENNY

NGA No.	CIVIL PARISH	TOWNLAND OR TOWN, STREET	OS No.	CHURCH	GRAVE-YARD
1	Abbeyleix				
2	Aghaviller	Aghaviller	31		G
		Hugginstown	31,35	RC	G
		Newmarket	31	RC	
3	Aglish				
4	Aharney	Ballyconra	4,5, 9		G
		Lisdowney	4,9	RC	
5	Arderra				
6	Attanagh	Earlsgarden	5	RC	
7	Balleen				
8	Ballinamara	Ballycannon	13,18	EC	G
9	Ballybur				
10	Ballycallan	Ballycallan	18,22	Old RC (part of)	
				EC	G
		Ballyhack	18	RC (part of)	
		Gorteenteen	18	RC	
		Michaelschurch	18,19		G
11	Ballygurrim	Jamestown	41		G
12	Ballylarkin				
13	Ballylinch	Ballylinch Demesne	8		G
14	Ballytarsney	Ballytarsney	42		G
15	Ballytobin	Caherlesk	26,27, 31	EC	
16	Blackrath	Maddockstown	20		G
17	Blanchvilleskill	Blanchvillestown	20,24		G
18	Borrismore				
19	Burnchurch	Burnchurch	23	EC	G
20	Callan	Callan, Green Street	26	RC	
		Mill Street	26	EC	G
				Friary RC	
		Kilbride Glebe	26		G
21	Castlecomer	Ardra	5,6	EC	G
		Castlecomer, Bowden's Row	5	M	

125

NGA No.	CIVIL PARISH	TOWNLAND OR TOWN, STREET	OS No.	CHURCH	GRAVE- YARD
21	Castlecomer	Castlecomer, Kilkenny Street	5	RC Convent RC	
		Clogh	2	RC	
		Coolbaun	6	M	
		Gorteen	6	EC M	G
		Moneenroe	6	RC	G
22	Castleinch or Inchyolaghan	Castleinch or Inchyolaghan	19,23	EC	G
23	Clara	Churchclara	20		G
		Rathgarvan or Clifden	20	RC	
24	Clashacrow	Clashacrow	13		G
25	Clomantagh	Clomantagh Lower	9,12, 13		G
		Woodsgift	13	EC	G
26	Clonamery	Ballygub New	33	RC	
		Clonamery	33		G
27	Clonmore	Clonmore	42		G
		Graigavine	42	EC	
28	Columbkille	Columbkille	28		G
		Kilcullen	28,32		G
29	Coolaghmore	Coolaghmore	26,30	RC	G
30	Coolcashin	Coolcashin	9	RC	G
31	Coolcraheen	Shanganny	10		G
32	Danesfort	Annamult	23,24 27,28		G
		Danesfort	23		G
		Dundaryark	23	RC	
33	Derrynahinch	Town of Ballyhale	31,32	RC	G
		Castlegannon	35,36		G
34	Donaghmore	Ballyragget, Castle Street	10	RC	
		Donaghmore	10		G
		Sraleagh	5		G
35	Dunbell				
36	Dungarvan	Dungarvan	24	EC	G

NGA No.	CIVIL PARISH	TOWNLAND OR TOWN, STREET	OS No.	CHURCH	GRAVE-YARD
36	Dungarvan	Dungarvan Glebe	24	RC	
37	Dunkitt	Dunkitt	43		G
		Rathnasmolagh	40,43	RC	G
38	Dunmore	Dunmore	14	EC	G
39	Dunnamaggan	Danganmore	31		G
		Dunnamaggan East	27,31		G
		Dunnamaggan West		RC	
40	Durrow	Ballynaslee	4		G
41	Dysart	Coan West	11	RC	
					G
		Dysart Glebe	10		G
		Smithstown	6	RC	
42	Dysartmoon	Ballyneale	37		G
		Curraghlane	36,37	RC	
43	Earlstown	Newtown (Baker)	23,27		G
		Newtown (Shea)	27	RC	
44	Ennisnag	Ennisnag	23,27	EC	G
45	Erke	Bayswell	7,8		G
		Garrylaun	3,8	EC	G
		Lough	8	RC	
		Moneynamuck	3,8		G
				RC	G
		Whiteswall	3		G
					G
46	Famma				
47	Fertagh	Donaghmore Upper	8		G
		Grangefertagh	8		G
		Johnstown, Chapel Street	8	RC	
		Church Street		EC	G
48	Fiddown	Ardclone	39	RC	
		Fiddown	39	EC	G
		Oldcourt	39	RC	G
49	Freshford	Freshford, Kilkenny Street	13	EC	G
		Market Square		RC	

NGA No.	CIVIL PARISH	TOWNLAND OR TOWN, STREET	OS No.	CHURCH	GRAVE-YARD
50	Garranamanagh				
51	Gaulskill	Ballynamorahan	43	EC	G
52	Glashare	Glashare	3,8		G
53	Gowran	Blanchvillespark	20		G
		Gowran	20	RC	
		Gowran, Main Street	20	EC	G
54	Graiguenamanagh	Graiguenamanagh	29	EC	
		Graiguenamanagh, Chapel Street	29	RC	G
		Oldgrange	25,29		G
55	Grange	Church Hill	23	RC	G
56	Grangekilree	Wallslough	23		G
57	Grangemaccomb	Connahy	10	RC	
		Grange	9		G
58	Grangesilvia	Barrowmount	21,25		G
		Duninga	21		G
		Goresbridge, Back Road	21	RC	
		Grange Lower	21,25	EC	G
		Grange Upper	21,25		G
59	Inistioge	Inistioge, Church Street	32	RC	
				EC	G
		Main Street		M	
60	Jerpointabbey	Jerpointabbey	28,32		G
61	Jerpointchurch	Coolroebeg	28,32	RC	
		Jerpointchurch	28,32		G
		Kilvinoge	28,32		G
62	Jerpointwest				
63	Kells	Glebe	27	EC	
					G
		Town of Kells	27	RC	
		Kellsgrange	23,27	RC	
		Rathduff (Madden)	27		G
64	Kilbeacon	Garrandarragh	40	RC	G
				EC	G

NGA No.	CIVIL PARISH	TOWNLAND OR TOWN, STREET	OS No.	CHURCH	GRAVE-YARD
65	Kilbride	Kilbride	40,41		G
66	Kilcoan				
67	Kilcolumb	Rathinure	44		G
68	Kilcooly				
69	Kilculliheen				
70	Kilderry				
71	Kilfane	Blessington	28,29	RC	
		Kilfane West	24,28	EC	G
72	Kilferagh	Kilferagh	19,20, 23		G
		Sheastown	19,20 23,24		G
73	Kilkeasy	Kilkeasy	31,35 36		G
		Knockmoylan	35	RC	
74	Kilkieran				
75	Killahy	Greenhill	13		G
		Killahy	35		G
76	Killaloe	Killaloe	22	RC	G
77	Killamery	Killamery	30	EC	G
		Meallaghmore Upper	30	RC	G
		Oldcastle Lower	30,34		G
		Rossaneny (Reade)	30		G
78	Killarney				
79	Kilmacahill	Kilmacahill	20,20	EC	G
80	Kilmacar	Kilmacar	10		G
81	Kilmacow	Kilmacow	43	EC	G
		Narrabaun South	43		G
82	Kilmademoge	Kilmademoge	14		G
		Mohill	14		G
83	Kilmadum	Ballyfoyle	14,15	RC	G
84	Kilmaganny	Kilmaganny, Chapel Street	31	RC	G
		Church Street		EC	G

NGA No.	CIVIL PARISH	TOWNLAND OR TOWN, STREET	OS No.	CHURCH	GRAVE-YARD
85	Kilmakevogue	Graiguenakill	41		G
		Robinstown	41	RC	G
86	Kilmanagh	Kilmanagh	18,22	EC	G
		Pottlerath	18,22	RC	
87	Kilmenan	Gorteenara	5		G
88	Kilree	Kilree	27		G
89	Knocktopher	Kilcurl (Anglesey)	31		G
		Town of Knocktopher	31	Friary RC	
					G
				EC	G
		Sheepstown	31		G
90	Lismateige				
91	Listerlin	Listerlin	36,37	RC	
92	Mallardstown	Mallardstown Great	26,27		G
93	Mayne	Jenkinstown	14		G
94	Mothell	Coolcullen	11	EC	G
		Lisnafunshin	10	RC	
95	Muckalee	Clogharinka	11	RC	
		Muckalee	10,11		G
96	Odagh	Leugh	13,14	RC	
		Odagh	14	EC	
		Threecastles	13,14		G
97	Outrath	Foulkstown	19,23	Old RC	
				New RC	
		Outrath	19,23		G
98	Owning	Owning	34,35		G
				RC	
99	Pleberstown				
100	Pollrone	Mooncoin, Chapel Street	42	RC	G
		Convent Street		Convent RC	
		Pollrone	42		G

NGA No.	CIVIL PARISH	TOWNLAND OR TOWN, STREET	OS No.	CHURCH	GRAVE-YARD
101	Portnascully	Licketstown	45	RC	G
		Portnascully	45		G
102	Powerstown	Powerstown East	25	EC	G
		Tomnahaha	25	RC	
103	Rathaspick				
104	Rathbeagh	Rathbeagh	9,10		G
105	Rathcoole	Carrigeen	15		G
		Mountnugent Lower	15	RC	G
106	Rathkieran	Rathkieran	42	EC	G
107	Rathlogan	Rathlogan	8		G
108	Rathpatrick	Kilmurry	43,46, 47	RC	G
		Rathpatrick	43,44		G
109	Rosbercon	Millbanks	37	RC	
		Town of Rosbercon	37	EC	G
110	Rosconnell	Castlemarket	1		G
111	Rossinan				
112	St. Canice's	Kilkenny, Black Abbey Street	19	RC	
		The Colonnade		St. Canice's EC	G
		Dean Street Upper		RC	
		New Road		RC	
		Walkin Street Upper			G
		Troyswood	14,19		G
113	St. John's	Kilkenny, Dublin Road	19	RC	G
		John Street Lower		EC	G
		Loughmerans	14,19	RC	
		Purcellsinch	19		G
		Radestown North	14		G
114	St. Martin's	Templemartin	20		G
115	St. Mary's	Kilkenny, James Street	19	RC	
				unfinished RC	
		Red Lane		Convent RC	
		St. Mary's Lane		EC	G

COUNTY KILKENNY

NGA No.	CIVIL PARISH	TOWNLAND OR TOWN, STREET	OS No.	CHURCH	GRAVE-YARD
115	St. Mary's	Kilkenny,Walkin Street Lower	19	Friary RC	
		William Street		M	
116	St. Maul's	Kilkenny, Green's Bridge Street	19		G
117	St. Patrick's	Kilkenny Chapel Lane	19	RC	
		Ormond Street		P	
		Patrick Street Upper			G
118	Shanbogh	Shanbogh Upper	37,41		G
119	Shankill	Kellymount	15,16, 20,21	RC	G
		Shankill	16,21	EC	
					G
120	Sheffin	Clontubbrid	9	RC	G
		Tifeaghna(Browne)	9		G
121	Stonecarthy	Stonecarthy East	27		G
		Town of Stoneyford	27	RC	G
122	The Rower	Carranroe Upper	33,37		G
		Farrantemple	33	EC	G
		Raheenduff	33,37	RC	
123	Thomastown	Cloghabrody	28		G
		Grennan	28,32		G
		Thomastown, Chapel Lane	28	RC	G
		Pipe Street		EC	G
124	Tibberaghny	Tibberaghny	38		G
125	Tiscoffin	Castlewarren	15	RC	
		Freneystown	15,20	EC	G
126	Treadingstown	Bennettsbridge	24	EC	G
127	Tubbrid	Tubbrid	39	RC	G
					G
128	Tubbridbritain	Garranconnell	12	RC	G
		Kildrinagh	12,13, 17		G
		Tubbrid Upper	12,13		G
129	Tullaghanbrogue	Grove	23		G
		Kilballykeefe	22		G

132

NGA No.	CIVIL PARISH	TOWNLAND OR TOWN, STREET	OS No.	CHURCH	GRAVE-YARD
130	Tullaherin	Tullaherin	24	RC	G
131	Tullahought	Kilmacoliver	34	RC	G
		Lamoge	30,34		G
132	Tullamaine	Tullamaine (Ashbrook)	22,23		G
133	Tullaroan	Tullaroan	18	RC	G
134	Ullard	Ullard	25	EC	G
135	Ullid	Ullid	42		G
136	Urlingford	Islands	8,12		G
		Urlingford, Main Street	12	RC	
137	Wells				
138	Whitechurch	Castletown	34,38		G
		Whitechurch	38	EC	G
139	Woolengrange	Rathcusack or Rathcorrig	24		G

NGA No.	CIVIL PARISH	TOWNLAND OR TOWN, STREET	OS No.	CHURCH	GRAVE-YARD
1	Annaduff	Aghamore	32,35	RC	
		Annaduff	32	EC	G
		Drumsna	31,32	RC	
2	Carrigallen	Carrigallen, Church Street	30	EC	G
		Drumeela	26,30	RC	G
		Errew	30,34		G
		Killygar	26,30	EC	
		Kivvy	30	P	G
		Newtowngore	26	EC	G
		Town of Newtowngore	26	M	
3	Cloonclare	Barrs West	8,12	RC	
		Cloonclare	11	Old EC	
		Kilmakerrill	12		G
		Town of Kiltyclogher	8	RC	
		Manorhamilton	7,11	EC	
		Town of Manorhamilton		M	
		Main Street		M	
		Old Church Street		EC	
		Tuckmillpark	11	RC	
4	Cloone	Aghavas	33	RC	
		Clooncumber	37,38	EC	
		Village of Cloone	33	RC	
				EC	
		Corduff North	29	EC	
		Farnaght	36	EC	G
		Gortletteragh	36	RC	
		Killyfea	29		G
		Lisgillock Glebe	29		G
5	Cloonlogher	Cloonlogher	11	Old EC	G
6	Drumlease	Town of Drumhaire	14	EC	
		Lugalustran	11	RC	
		Sriff	10		G
7	Drumreilly	Ardunsaghan	25	RC	G

NGA No.	CIVIL PARISH	TOWNLAND OR TOWN, STREET	OS No.	CHURCH	GRAVE-YARD
7	Drumreilly	Corraleehan	22	RC	G
		Cully	25,26	EC	
		Drumnafinnila	18,19	RC	
					G
		Fahy	18		G
		Lisroughty	22,25	RC	
8	Fenagh	Commons	25,29		G
		Drumlaheen	24,28	RC	
		Glebe	29	EC	G
9	Inishmagrath	Carrowlaur	18	RC	
		Corglass	20	RC	
		Curraghs South	20		G
		Derryvalannagher Glebe	18,20	RC	
		Town of Drumkeeran	17,18	M	
		Killadiskert	18		G
		Lavagh	17		G
		Sheena	17,18	EC	
10	Killanummery	Carrowcrin	14	RC	
		Killanummery	14,15	EC	
11	Killarga	Cornamarve	15	EC	
		Derrintawny	15	P	
		Killarga	15	RC	
12	Killasnet	Cartronatemple	7		G
		Diffreen	6,10		G
		Drumdillure	7	Episcopal Chapel	
		Drummans	7	Old RC	
		Gorteenguinnell	6,7	RC	
		Lugnafaughery	6	EC	G
		Mullies	7	RC	
		Nure	7		G
13	Kiltoghert	Carrick - on - Shannon Main Street	31	EC RC M	G

135

NGA No.	CIVIL PARISH	TOWNLAND OR TOWN, STREET	OS No.	CHURCH	GRAVE-YARD
13	Kiltoghert	Carrick - on - Shannon Main Street	31	M	
		Corlough	23		G
		Drumshanbo	23	RC	
		Town of Drumshanbo	23	EC M	G
		Gowel	27,28	RC	
		Town of Jamestown	31	RC	G
		Kiltoghert	27		G
		Lisdromarea North	28,32	EC	
14	Kiltubbrid	Corglass	24	EC	
		Kiltubbrid	24		G
		Roscarban	24	RC	
15	Mohill	Boeeshil	32		G
		Cavan	32	RC	
		Cloonmorris	37		G
		Cloonturk	35	RC	
		Corrabeagh	28	RC	
		Knockadrinan	37	RC	
		Mohill	32	RC	G
		Mohill, Main Street	32	EC M	G
16	Oughteragh	Ballinamore, Chapel Lane	25	RC	G
		Church Lane	25	EC	G
		Town of Ballinamore	25	M	
		Drumbibe	21,24	RC	G
		Oughteragh	25		G
17	Rossinver	Drummans	3		G
		Gubalaun	5		G
		Gubnageer	5	RC	
		Keeloges	3,4	RC	

NGA No.	CIVIL PARISH	TOWNLAND OR TOWN, STREET	OS No.	CHURCH	GRAVE-YARD
17	Rossinver	Village of Kinlough	2	RC	
				EC	
		Kinlough	2		G
		Tawnytallan	1	RC	

COUNTY LEIX (QUEEN'S COUNTY)

NGA No.	CIVIL PARISH	TOWNLAND OR TOWN, STREET	OS No.	CHURCH	GRAVE-YARD
1	Abbeyleix	Abbeyleix, Chapel Lane	24	RC	G
		Main Street	23,24	M	
		Market Street	24	BAP	
		Abbeyleix Demesne	29	EC	G
		Clonkeen	29,30		G
		Tullyroe	23	EC	G
2	Aghaboe	Aghaboe	22	EC	G
		Borris in Ossory, Chapel Lane	21,22	RC	G
		Knockaroe	22	RC	G
		Knockseera	22		G
		Lismore	22		G
		Park	29	RC	G
3	Aghmacart	Aghmacart	34	EC	G
		Ballynevin	34,35	RC	
		Toberboe or Killennymore	35		G
4	Aharney	Aharney	35		G
5	Ardea	Acragar	8		G
		Dangans	8		G
		Derrygile	8		G
		Portnahinch	4		G
6	Attanagh	Glebe	35	EC	G
7	Ballyadams	Ballintubbert	19	EC	G
		Ballyadams	19		G
		Monascreeban	19,20		G
8	Ballyroan	Ballyroan, Chapel Street	24	RC	
		Church Lane		EC	G
9	Bordwell	Bordwell Big	28		G
		Chapel Hill	28	RC	G
		Kilbreedy	28		G
10	Borris	Maryborough, Chapel Lane	13		G
		Church Lane			G
		Church Street		Z	
				M	
		Quality Row		EC	G

COUNTY LEIX (QUEEN 'S COUNTY)

NGA No.	CIVIL PARISH	TOWNLAND OR TOWN, STREET	OS No.	CHURCH	GRAVE-YARD
10	Borris	Maryborough, Ridge Road	13		G
11	Castlebrack	Castlebrack	1		G
		Clonaghadoo	3	RC	G
12	Clonenagh and Clonagheen	Ballyfin Demesne	12	EC	G
		Ballylusk	12		G
		Boghlone	12,13		G
		Boley Lower	23		G
		Clonadacasey	17	RC	
		Clonaddadoran	17,18		G
		Clondarrig	12		G
		Clonenagh	17		G
		Cromoge	23		G
		Derrykearn	23		G
		Knocknakearn	12	RC	
		Mountrath, Coote Street	16,17	Convent RC	
				RC	
		Main Street		EC	G
					G
		Maryborough Road		M	
		Miss Lalor's Lane		M	
		Thomas' Court		Q	
		Rosskelton	17	EC	G
		Shananoe	23	RC	
		Tinnakill	17	RC	G
13	Cloydagh				
14	Coolbanagher	Coolbanagher	8		G
		Killimy	8		G
		Morett	8,9	RC	G
				EC	G
15	Coolkerry	Coolkerry	28		G
16	Curraclone	Curraclone	14		G
		Monaferrick	14	EC	
17	Donaghmore	Donaghmore, The Fair Green	28	EC	G

COUNTY LEIX (QUEENS COUNTY)

NGA No.	CIVIL PARISH	TOWNLAND OR TOWN, STREET	OS No.	CHURCH	GRAVE-YARD
17	Donaghmore	Killadooley	28	RC	
18	Durrow	Durrow, George's Street	35	RC	G
		Patrick Street		M	
		The Square		EC	G
19	Dysartenos	Dysart	13		G
		Raheenanisky	18	RC	G
20	Dysartgallen	Aghnacross	30		G
		Ballinakill, Church Street	30	RC	
				EC	G
		Graiguenahowen	30	RC in progress	
		Kilcronan	30		G
					G
		Knockardague	30	RC	
21	Erke				
22	Fossy or Timahoe	Fossy Lower	18,19, 24,25		G
		Timahoe	18,19	RC	
23	Glashare				
24	Kilcolmanbane	Kilcolmanbane	18		G
		Kilvahan	18		G
25	Kilcolmanbrack	Cremorgan	18		G
26	Kildellig	Kildellig	22		G
27	Killabban	Ballylynan	26	RC	
		Ballynagall	26,32	RC	G
		Castletown	26	EC	G
		Kilgory	36		G
		Killabban	26		G
		Killeen	26,32	RC	G
		Mayo	31,36	EC	G
		Monavea	31,36	RC	G
		Rahin	25,26		G
28	Killenny	Killenny	13,14		G
29	Killermogh	Killermogh	29		G
		Rathmakelly Glebe	29	EC	G

COUNTY LEIX (QUEEN'S COUNTY)

NGA No.	CIVIL PARISH	TOWNLAND OR TOWN, STREET	OS No.	CHURCH	GRAVE-YARD
30	Killeshin	Graigue	32,37	EC	G
		Graigue, Maryborough Street	32,37	RC	
		Killeshin	32,37		G
				RC	G
		Leagh	32		G
		Olderrig	32,37		G
31	Kilmanman	Ballynahown	6		G
		Clonaslee, Chapel Lane	2	RC	
		Main Street		EC	
		Kilmanman	2		G
32	Kilteale	Ballycarroll	13	EC	
		Great Heath	13		G
				RC	G
		Kilteale	13,14		G
33	Kyle	Kyle	15,21		G
34	Lea	Ballyadding	9		G
		Ballycarroll	5,9	RC	G
		Loughmansland Glebe	5		G
		Portarlington, French Church Street	4,5	EC	G
		Market Square		EC	
		Rathmiles	5,9		G
		Tirhogar	5		G
35	Monksgrange	Grange	26,32		G
36	Moyanna	Moyanna	14		G
		Vicarstown (Cosby)	14	RC	
37	Offerlane	Camross	16	RC	G
		Churchtown	16		G
		Elderfield	16	RC	
		Glebe	16	EC	G
		Knockbrack	16,22	RC	G
		Lacka	11	EC	G
		Mountainfarm	11	RC	
38	Rathaspick	Crissard	25,31	RC	
		Doonane	31	RC	G

141

NGA No.	CIVIL PARISH	TOWNLAND OR TOWN, STREET	OS No.	CHURCH	GRAVE-YARD
38	Rathaspick	Rathaspick	25		
39	Rathdowney	Ballybuggy	28,34		G
		Clonfeeb	33,39		G
		Errill	27		G
		Garryduff	27		G
		Rathdowney, Brewery Lane	28	M	
		Chapel Street		RC	
		Church Street		EC	G
40	Rathsaran	Eglish	27	EC	G
		Mountoliver	28	RC	
41	Rearymore				
42	Rosconnell				
43	Rosenallis	Ballyhuppahane	7	M	
		Capard	7	RC	
		Graigue	3	RC	
		Village of Rosenallis	3	EC	G
		Tinneel	3		G
		Mountmellick, Church Lane	8	M	
		Church Square		EC	G
				M	
		Market Square		Q	
44	St. John's				
45	Shrule	Shrule	32		G
46	Skirk	Skirk or Newtown	21	EC	G
47	Sleaty	Sleaty	32		G
48	Straboe	Ballydavis	13		G
		Straboe	13		G
49	Stradbally	Carricksallagh	19		G
		Stradbally, Chapel Lane	19	RC	
		Main Street		EC	G
				M	
		Market Square		M	
50	Tankardstown	Shanganaghmore	20,26	RC	G
		Tankardstown	26		G

NGA No.	CIVIL PARISH	TOWNLAND OR TOWN, STREET	OS No.	CHURCH	GRAVE- YARD
51	Tecolm	Corbally	25		G
52	Timogue	Timogue	19	EC	G
53	Tullomoy	Clopook	19		G
		Luggacurren	19,25	RC	
		Tullomoy	19		G

COUNTY LIMERICK

NGA No.	CIVIL PARISH	TOWNLAND OR TOWN, STREET	OS No.	CHURCH	GRAVE-YARD
1	Abbeyfeale	Abbeyfeale East	42,51	EC	
		Abbeyfeale West	42		Childrens G
		Abbeyfeale, Main Street	42	RC in ruins	G
		New Street	42	RC	
		Crag	52		G
		Killkinlea Lower	42,57		G
2	Abington	Abbington	14,15	EC	G
		Annagh	6		G
		Liscreagh	7	RC	
		Sandylane	14	RC	
3	Adare	Adare	21		G
		Town of Adare, Main Street	21		G
		Blackabbey	21	EC	
		Gortaganniff	21	M	
		Tuogh	20,21		G
4	Aglishcormick	Ballynagally	24		G
5	Anhid	Anhid East	30		G
6	Ardagh	Ministers Land	28	RC	G
7	Ardcanny	Mellon	4		G
8	Ardpatrick	Ardpatrick	56		G
9	Askeaton	Askeaton	11	EC	G
		Cloonreask	10,11	RC	
		Moig South	10,11		G
10	Athlacca	Athlacca South	39	EC	G
		Rathcannon	31,39	RC	
11	Athneasy	Adamstown	40		G
		Ballinvana	40,48		G
		Martinstown	48	RC	
12	Ballinard	Village of Herbertstown	32	RC	G
13	Ballingaddy	Ballingaddy North	47,48	RC	G

144

NGA No.	CIVIL PARISH	TOWNLAND OR TOWN, STREET	OS No.	CHURCH	GRAVE-YARD
14	Ballingarry	Ballingarry	49	RC	
					G
		Ballygrennan	38		G
		Cloontemple	29,37	EC	G
		Glenlary	48,49		G
		Granagh	38	RC	
				Old EC	
					G
		Kilmacon	30		G
		Morenane	30,38		G
		Rylanes	29	RC	
15	Ballinlough	Ballinlough	32,33		G
16	Ballybrood	Ballybrood Village	23	EC	G
		Rockfarm	23	RC	
17	Ballycahane	Ballycahane Upper	22	EC	G
18	Ballylanders	Ballylanders	49		G
				EC Unfinished	
					G
		Village of Ballylanders	49	EC	
				RC	
		Cullane North	57		G
19	Ballynaclogh	Ballynaclogh	24		G
20	Ballynamona	Ballynamona	32		G
21	Ballyscaddan	Ryves Castle	41		G
22	Bruff	Bruff, Fair Green Road	31,32, 40	RC	
		Main Street		EC	G
		Newtown	31,32		G
23	Bruree	Ballyfookeen	38,39	RC	
		Ballynoe	39	EC	G
		Town of Bruree	39	RC	
		Howardstown North	39		G
24	Caheravally	Drombanny	13	RC	
		Raheen	13		G

NGA No.	CIVIL PARISH	TOWNLAND OR TOWN, STREET	OS No.	CHURCH	GRAVE-YARD
25	Caherconlish	Village of Caherconlish, Main Street	14,23	EC	G
		Castle-Erkin South	14,15		G
26	Cahercorney	Cahercorney	23,32	EC	G
27	Caherelly	Ballybricken North	23	EC	
		Caherelly West	23		G
28	Cahernarry	Cahernarry (Cripps)	13,14	EC	G
29	Cappagh	Cappagh	2		G
30	Carrigparson	Carrigparson	14		G
		Srahane	14	RC	
31	Castletown	Carrig Beg	24,25		G
32	Chapelrussell	Pallas	3,11	M	
				EC	G
33	Clonagh	Clonagh	28		G
		Coolcappagh	19,28	RC	
34	Cloncagh	Cloncagh	37	RC	
					G
35	Cloncrew	Cloncrew	45,54		G
36	Clonelty	Village of Knockaderry	28,29, 36,37	RC	
37	Clonkeen	Clonkeen (Barrington)	6,14		G
38	Clonshire	Clonshire More	20,21		G
39	Colmanswell	Foxhall West	46	RC	
		Gortroe	46		G
40	Corcomohide	Village of Ballyagran	46	RC	
		Castletown	38,46		G
		Gortroe	37,38, 45	EC	
41	Crecora	Ballyveelish	22	RC	
		Glebe	22		G
42	Croagh	Adamswood	29		G
		Croagh	20	EC	
43	Croom	Cloonanna	12,21		G
		Croom	30	EC RC	G

NGA No.	CIVIL PARISH	TOWNLAND OR TOWN, STREET	OS No.	CHURCH	GRAVE-YARD
43	Croom	Dohora	30,38	RC	
		Dunnaman	21,30		G
44	Darragh	Darragh More	56,57, 59		G
		Spittle	56,57	RC	
45	Derrygalvin	Ballysimon (Dickson)	5,13		G
46	Donaghmore	Bohereen	13	RC	
		Drombanny	13		G
47	Doon	Googa Upper	15,16	RC	
		Doon South	16	EC	G
48	Doondonnell	Cloghanarold	20,29		G
49	Drehidtarsna	Drehidtarsna	21	EC	
50	Dromin	Dromin South	39	RC	G
51	Dromkeen	Dromkeen South	23,24	EC RC	G
52	Dromcolliher	Dromcolliher, Chapel Street (East Side)	54		G
		Chapel Street (West Side)		RC	
53	Dunmoylan				
54	Dysert				
55	Effin	Effin	47,55		G
		Garrynderk	47	RC	
		Tobernea West	47,55	RC	
56	Emlygrennan	Balline	48		G
57	Fedamore	Ballyea	22	RC	
		Fedamore	22	EC	G
		Rockstown	23		G
58	Galbally	Duntryleague	41,49	EC	G
		Galbally	49	EC	G
		Village of Lowes Town	49	RC	
59	Glenogra	Crean	31		G
		Glenogra	22,31		G

NGA No.	CIVIL PARISH	TOWNLAND OR TOWN, STREET	OS No.	CHURCH	GRAVE-YARD
59	Glenogra	Meanus	31	RC	
60	Grange	Grange Lower	23,36		G
61	Grean	Garranemore	24	EC	
		Village of Nicker	24	RC	
		Pallas	24		G
62	Hackmys				
63	Hospital	Barrysfarm	32,40	RC	G
64	Inch St. Lawrence	Inch St. Lawrence North	14,23	RC	
65	Iverruss	Ballycanauna	3,11	RC	
		Beagh	3		G
66	Kilbehany	Anglesborough	57,58	RC	
		Churchquarter	58	EC	G
		Knockrour	58,60	RC	
67	Kilbolane				
68	Kilbradan	Kilbradan	19		G
69	Kilbreedy-Major	Ballygrennan	40,48	RC	
		Kilbreedy East	48		G
70	Kilbreedy-Minor	Kilbreedy	47		G
71	Kilcolman	Kilcolman	19	RC	
					G
72	Kilcornan	Blossomhill	11	RC	
		Cowpark	11		G
		Kilbreedy	11,12 20,21		G
					G
		Moig East Glebe	11		G
				EC	
		Stonehall	11	RC in ruins	
73	Kilcullane	Kilcullane	32		G
74	Kildimo	Curraheen	11,12	RC	
		Kildimo	12	RC	
				EC	G
75	Kilfergus	Glin Demesne	17	EC	
		Town of Glin, Chapel Street	17,18	RC	

NGA No.	CIVIL PARISH	TOWNLAND OR TOWN, STREET	OS No.	CHURCH	GRAVE-YARD
76	Kilfinnane	Town of Kilfinnane	48,56	EC RC	G
77	Kilfinny	Ballynakill	30		G
		Village of Kilfinny	30	RC	
78	Kilflyn	Abbey	56		G
		Ballyorgan	56	EC RC	G
79	Kilfrush	Kilfrush	40,41		G
80	Kilkeedy	Ballyanrahan West	12	RC	
		Ballybrown	12	RC	
		Glebe	12	EC	G
81	Killagholehane	Village of Broadford	44,45 52,54	RC	
		Lackagh Lower	54		G
		Springfield	43,54	EC	G
82	Killeedy	Gartnaclohy	44,53	EC RC	
		Killeedy North	44		G
		Rahanagh (Detached)	36,44	RC	
		Raheenagh	44	RC	
		Toornafulla	43,52	RC	
83	Killeely	Ballynanty Beg	5		G
		Coonagh West	4,5		Childrens G
		Glebe	5		G
84	Killeenagarrif	Biddyford	6	RC	
		Killeenagarriff	6		G
85	Killeenoghty	Killeenoghty	22		G
86	Killonahan	Killonahan	21,22		G
87	Kilmeedy	Village of Feenagh	45	RC	
		Village of Kilmeedy	37,45	RC	
		Pallas	37,45		G
88	Kilmoylan	Ballyhahill	18	RC	
		Kilmoylan	19		G

COUNTY LIMERICK

NGA No.	CIVIL PARISH	TOWNLAND OR TOWN, STREET	OS No.	CHURCH	GRAVE-YARD
89	Kilmurry	Killonan	6,14		G
		Newcastle	5,6,	EC	G
		Newtown	5,6	RC	
90	Kilpeacon	Kilpeacon	22	EC	G
91	Kilquane	Ballyhaght	55		G
92	Kilscannell	Killeheen	28,29	M	
		Kilscannell	28	EC	G
93	Kilteely	Village of Kilteely	33	RC	G
94	Knockainy	Ballynagallagh	32		G
		Knockainy West	32,40	RC	G
				EC	G
		Loughgur	32		G
		Patrickswell	32	RC	G
					G
95	Knocklong	Ballynahinch	40,48		G
		Knocklong East	40,41		G
		Knocklong West	41	RC	
96	Knocknagaul	Lemonfield	13		G
97	St. John's	Limerick, Johns Square	5	St.Johns EC	G
		New Clare Street		RC	
		Nicholas Street		St.Johns RC	
		Suburbs of Limerick, Pennywell	5		G
98	St. Lawrence's	Suburbs of Limerick, Green Hill	5		G
99	St. Mary's	Limerick, Chapel Lane	5	St.Marys RC	
		Convent Street			Quakers G
		Creagh Lane		Old RC	
		Quay Lane		St.Marys P	
100	St. Michael's	Ballinacurra (Bowman)	5		Quakers G
		Limerick, Barrington Street	5	St.Michael EC	

NGA No.	CIVIL PARISH	TOWNLAND OR TOWN, STREET	OS No.	CHURCH	GRAVE-YARD
100	St. Michael's	Limerick, Bedford Row	5	M I	
		Boxborough Road (City Place)		RC	
		Catherine Street		Episcopal Chapel	
		Cecil Street Upper		Q	
		Church Yard Lane			St. Michaels G
		Denmark Street Lower		St. Michaels RC	
		Georges Street		M	
				Augustinian RC	
		Glentworth Street Upper		Dominican RC	
				P	
		Henry Street		Franciscan RC	
		Mallow Street		D	
		Sexton Street		Nunnery RC Attached	
		Rossbrien	13		G
101	St. Munchin's	Clonconane	5		G
		Limerick, Barrack Street	5	RC attached to Convent	
		Church Street		St. Munchins EC	G
102	St. Nicholas'	Limerick North Strand	5	RC	
103	St. Patrick's	Singland	5		G
104	Lismakeery	Lismakeery	19,20		G
105	Loghill	Kilfergus	17,18		G
		Loghill	9,18	EC	G
				RC	

NGA No.	CIVIL PARISH	TOWNLAND OR TOWN, STREET	OS No.	CHURCH	GRAVE-YARD
106	Ludden	Ludden Beg	14,23		G
107	Mahoonagh	Appletown	44,45	RC	
					G
		Mahoonagh	36		G
		Village of Mahoonagh	36	RC	
108	Monagay	Glebe	36		G
		Newcastle, Knockaun Road	58	Convent	
				RC	
		Convent Ground		RC	
		Templeglentan East	48	RC	
		Templeglentan West	53		G
109	Monasteranenagh	Camus North	31		G
		Knocknagranshy	22,31	RC	
		Monaster South	31		G
		Sixmilebridge	22,23 31,32	RC	G
110	Morgans	Morgans North	20		G
111	Mungret	Ballycummin	13	RC	
		Dromdarrig	13	EC	G
112	Nantinan	Ballingarrane	20	M	
		Ballyhomock	20	RC	
		Nantinan	92	EC	G
		Rathnaseer	29		G
113	Newcastle	Churchtown	36		G
		Gortboy	36		Union Workhouse G
		Town of Newcastle, Square	36	EC	
114	Oola	Glebe	24,25		G
				M	
		Moanoola	23	RC	
115	Particles	Sunville Upper	56	RC	
116	Rathjordan	Rathjordan	23,32		G
117	Rathkeale	Ballyallinan North	29		G
		Kilcolman East	29,37		G

NGA No.	CIVIL PARISH	TOWNLAND OR TOWN, STREET	OS No.	CHURCH	GRAVE-YARD
117	Rathkeale	Kyletown	20,29		G
		Town of Rathkeale	29	RC	
		Rathkeale, Church Street	29	EC	G
118	Rathronan	Village of Athea	34	RC	
		Glenville	25	EC	G
		Templeathea West	26,27, 34,35		G
119	Robertstown	Knockpatrick	10		G
		Robertstown	10,19	RC	
120	Rochestown	Rochestown	22,23		G
121	St. Peter's and St. Paul's				
122	Shanagolden	Clashganniff	19	RC	
		Shanagolden Demesne	10,19	EC	
123	Stradbally	Village of Montpelier, Castleconnell Road	1		G
		Stradbally North, Castleview	1,5	RC	
		Stradbally North, Shannon Lodge	5	EC	G
124	Tankardstown	Tankardstown Sough	47		G
125	Templebredon	Templebredon	33		G
126	Tomdeely				
127	Tullabracky	Rockbarton	31,32	EC	
		Tullabracky	31,32		G
128	Tuogh	Tuogh	15	EC	G
		Turagh	15	RC	
129	Tuoghcluggin	Castleluggin	24		G
130	Uregare	Uregare	39,40		G

COUNTY LONDONDERRY

NGA No.	CIVIL PARISH	TOWNLAND OR TOWN, STREET	OS No.	CHURCH	GRAVE-YARD
1	Aghadowey	Aghadowey	11,18	EC	G
		Ballylintagh	11	P	G
		Ballymenagh	11	P	G
		Ballywillin	11,18	P	G
		Killeague	11	P	G
		Mullaghinch	18,19	RC	
2	Aghanloo	Drumbane	5,6,9	EC	G
		Rathfad	5,6		G
3	Agivey	Mullaghmore	12		G
4	Arboe	Ballygonny More	48	P	
		Drummullan	48	RC	
5	Artrea	Ballyeglish	46,47,49		G
		Ballymaguigan	42,47	MO	G
		Ballymulligan	47	P	
		Ballynenagh	46,47	RC	
		Derrygarve	42	RC	G
		Drumenagh	47		G
		Lisnamarrow	47	EC	G
		Moneymore	46,48	RC	G
		Moneymore, Hammond Road	46,48	P	
		Stonard Street		P	
6	Ballinderry	Ballinderry	49	M	G
		Ballylifford	49	RC	G
		Killymuck	49	EC	
7	Ballyaghran	Glebe	3		G
		Portstewart, Church Street	3	P	
		Main Street		M	
8	Ballymoney				
9	Ballynascreen	Cavanreagh	40	EC	G
		Town of Draperstown	40	P	
		Moneyconey	39,40		G

154

NGA No.	CIVIL PARISH	TOWNLAND OR TOWN, STREET	OS No.	CHURCH	GRAVE-YARD
9	Ballynascreen	Moneyneany	35	RC	
		Moykeeran	40	EC	G
		Straw	40	RC	G
		Tullybrick	40,45	RC	
10	Ballyrashane	Glebe	8	EC	G
		Kirkistown	8	P	
11	Ballyscullion	Bellaghy, Castle-Dawson Street	37	P	
		Church Lane		EC	G
		Church Island	42		G
		Tamlaghtduff	37	RC	G
		Tamniaran	42	EC	
12	Ballywillin	Ballymaclevennon West	3	P	
		Glebe	3		G
13	Balteagh	Ardmore	10,17	EC	G
		Drumsurn Lower	17	RC	
		Lislane	17	P	G
14	Banagher	Ballyhanedin	30	P	
		Fincarn	30	RC	G
		Magheramore	30,31		G
		Rallagh	30	EC	G
15	Bovevagh	Ballymoney	24,30	RC	G
		Bovevagh	24,26		G
				EC	G
		Camnish	24,26	P	G
		Gortnahey More	24	RC	
16	Carrick	Ballydarrog	16	I	
		Carrick East	16,17	EC	
		Largy	16	P	G
17	Clondermot	Altnagelvin	20	EC	G
				1st P	
				2nd P	
		Ballyshasky	21,22		G
		Clondermot	20		G
		Currynierin	20,22	RC	G

NGA No.	CIVIL PARISH	TOWNLAND OR TOWN, STREET	OS No.	CHURCH	GRAVE-YARD
17	Clondermot	Drumahoe	20	COV	
		Gortnessy	14	P	G
		Londonderry, Bond's Hill	20	COV	
		Chapel Road	20	RC	
		Primity	20	M	
		Templetown	14		G
18	Coleraine	Ballyclaber	7	P	
		Coleraine, Church Street	7	EC	G
		Circular Road		M	
		Long Commons		RC	
		Meeting House Place		BAP	
				P	
		New Row		P	
				CON	
		Taylors Row		M	
		Terrace Row		P	
19	Cumber Lower	Brackfield	22	P	
		Killaloo	22	EC	G
		Mullaboy	22,23	RC	G
20	Cumber Upper	Village of Clady	23	RC	G
		Cregg	23	P	
		Cumber	23	EC	G
21	Derryloran				
22	Desertlyn	Ballymully	46		G
		Carndaisy	46	BAP	
		Moneymore, Lawford Street	46		G
				M	
		Smith Street	46	EC	G
23	Desertmartin	Annagh and Moneysterlin	41		G
		Cullion	41	RC	G
		Town of Desertmartin	41	RC	G
					G
		Dromore	41	EC	G

NGA No.	CIVIL PARISH	TOWNLAND OR TOWN, STREET	OS No.	CHURCH	GRAVE- YARD
23	Desertmartin	Lecumpher	41	P	
24	Desertoghill	Ballynameen	18,26		G
		Craigavole	26	RC	
		Moneydig	18,19, 26,27	P	G
		Moyletra Kill	26	EC	G
25	Drumachose	Coolessan	9	P	G
		Derry Beg	10	COV	
		Derry More	10	P	
		Drummond	10		G
		Newtownlimavady (Alias) Ratbrady Beg	9	RC	
		Newtownlimavady, Irish Green	9	I	
				P	
		Main Street		CB	
				M	
				EC	G
		Meeting House Lane		U	
		Rathbrady More	9	P	
				P	
				P	G
26	Dunboe	Village of Articlave	2,3, 6,7	EC	G
				P	G
		Downhill	2	Temple used as RC	
27	Dungiven	Dungiven	24,25, 30,31	EC	G
				RC	
					G
		Dungiven, New Street	24,25, 30,31	P	
		Gartgarn	25	RC	G
		Scriggan	25	P	

NGA No.	CIVIL PARISH	TOWNLAND OR TOWN, STREET	OS No.	CHURCH	GRAVE-YARD
28	Errigal	Ballintemple	17,18, 25,26		G
		Boleran	18	RC	
		Brockagh	17,25, 26	RC	
		Garvagh	18	EC	G
		Garvagh, Main Street	18	2nd P	G
				P	
		Meeting House Lane		1st P	G
29	Faughanvale	Cregan	15	RC	
		Faughanvale	15		G
		Muff	14,15	EC	G
		Tullanee	15	P	
30	Formoyle	Ballinrees	6,7	P	
		Formoyle	6,10	EC	
31	Kilcronaghan	Mormeal	41	Old EC	G
		Tobermore, Main Street	36	P	G
				EC	
				BAP	
32	Kildollagh	Fishloughan	7,8	EC	G
33	Killelagh	Glebe	52	EC	
		Granaghan	32	RC	G
		Town of Swatragh	26,52	P	
		Tirhugh	32	EC	
34	Killowen	Churchland	7	RC	G
		Coleraine, Killowen Street	7	EC	G
35	Kilrea	Kilrea, Church Street	27	1st P	G
			27	EC	G
		Maghera Street		2nd P	G
36	Learmount	Altinure Upper	29,30	RC	
		Gortscreagan	29	RC	G
		Straid	23,29, 30		G
		Tireighter	29,30	EC	G
37	Lissan	Clagan	45,46	P	

NGA No.	CIVIL PARISH	TOWNLAND OR TOWN, STREET	OS No.	CHURCH	GRAVE-YARD
37	Lissan	Tullynure	45,46, 48	RC	
				EC	
38	Macosquin	Ballylagan	11,12	COV	G
		Camus	7,11,12		G
		Camus Macosquin Glebe	7	EC	
		Crossgare	11	P	G
		Englishtown	11	P	
		Ringrash More	7	COV	
39	Maghera	Culnady	32,33, 36,37	P	
		Village of Curran	36,37, 41,42	P	
		Fallagloon	31,32, 35,36	RC	G
		Maghera, Brewery Lane	36	M	
					G
				P	
		Main Street		EC	
					G
		Moyagall	37	RC	
40	Magherafelt	Aghagaskin	42	RC	
		Castledawson, Barrack Brae	42	M	
		Main Street		P	G
		Townparks of Magherafelt	41,42		G
		Magherafelt, Castledawson Street	41,42	EC	G
				M	
		Churchwell Street			G
		Meeting House Street		P	G
41	Tamlaght	Tamlaght	48,49	EC	G
42	Tamlaght Finlagan	Village of Ballykelly	9		G
		Drumond	9	EC	G
				P	
		Lomond	9	P	

NGA No.	CIVIL PARISH	TOWNLAND OR TOWN, STREET	OS No.	CHURCH	GRAVE-YARD
42	Tamlaght Finlagan	Mulkeeragh	9		G
		Oghill	9,16	RC	G
43	Tamlaght O'Crilly	Bovedy	26,27	SP	
				P	G
		Drumagarner	27	RC	G
		Drumard	33	P	G
		Drumlane	33	P	
		Drumnacanon	33	EC	G
		Inishrush	33	RC	G
		Tyanee	33	EC	G
44	Tamlaghtard or Magilligan	Duncrun	5,6	EC	G
		Margymonaghan	5	P	
		Tamlaght	5	RC	G
45	Templemore	Ballymagowan	20		G
		Culmore	13,14		G
		Killea	20		G
		Londonderry, Artillery Lane	20	4th P	
		Bridge Street		I	
		The Diamond		CB	
		East Wall		M	
		Fountain Street		RP	
		Great James Street		RC un-finished	
				CON	
				3rd P	
		Infirmary Road		EC	
		Lecky Road		RC	
		Lonemoor Street			G
		Long Tower		RC	G
		Magazine Street		M	
		Meeting House Row		EC	G
				1st P	

COUNTY LONDONDERRY

NGA No.	CIVIL PARISH	TOWNLAND OR TOWN, STREET	OS No.	CHURCH	GRAVE-YARD
45	Templemore	Londonderry, Pump Street	20	Convent RC	
		Queen Street		COV	
		St. Columbs Court		St.Columbs EC	G
		Strand Road		2nd P	
		Shantallow	13	P	G
46	Termoneeny	Cabragh	37,42	EC	
		Derganagh	36,37	SP	
		Mullagh	36		G

COUNTY LONGFORD

NGA No.	CIVIL PARISH	TOWNLAND OR TOWN, STREET	OS No.	CHURCH	GRAVE-YARD
1	Abbeylara	Abbeylara	11	RC	G
				EC	
		Ballinrooey	6,10	RC	
		Inchmore	6		G
2	Abbeyshrule	Abbeyshrule	23,24 27		G
		Drumanure	23	RC	
3	Agharra	Agharra	23,24		G
4	Ardagh	Cross	19	RC	
		Lyanmore	19	EC	
5	Ballymacormick	Ballinamore	18		G
		Curry	18	EC	
6	Cashel	Cashel	21	EC	
					G
		Cornadowagh	21,22	RC	
7	Clonbroney	Village of Ballinalee	9	RC	
		Clonbroney	10		G
		Drummeel	9,10 14,15	RC	G
		Gorteenrevagh	9	EC	G
		Lisraghtigan	10,15	P	
		Moatfarrell	14,15		G
8	Clongesh	Town of Newtownforbes	8	M	
				RC	
				EC	G
		St. Annes Glebe	8		G
9	Columkille	Aghnacliff	6	RC	G
		Cloonagh	6	RC	G
		Rathmore	5,6	EC	
10	Forgney	Clooncallow	27		G
		Forgney	27	EC	G
					G
				RC	
11	Granard	Carragh	10,11		G
				RC	G

COUNTY LONGFORD

NGA No.	CIVIL PARISH	TOWNLAND OR TOWN, STREET	OS No.	CHURCH	GRAVE-YARD
11	Granard	Granardkill	10	RC	G
		Granard, The Hill	10	EC	G
		Moxham Street		RC	
12	Kilcommock	Cartronawar	22	RC	
		Keenagh	22	EC	
		Keenagh, Ardagh Road	22	M	
		Kilcommock Glebe	22		G
13	Kilglass	Ballycloghan	19	RC	
		Glebe	19,23	EC	
					G
		Smithfield	23,24	RC	
14	Killashee	Aghnaskea	18	RC	
		Ballynakill	12,13		G
		Cloondara	8,13	RC	G
		Killashee and Aghakeeran	18	M	
		Templeton Glebe	18	EC	G
15	Killoe	Ballyduffy	1,2,3	RC	
		Corboy	14	P	
		Cornacullew	2		G
		Drumlish	5	RC	
				EC	
		Enybegs	9	RC	
		Killoe Glebe	9,14	EC	
		Killyfad	9,14	RC	
		Kilmahon	5		G
		Leggagh	2,3	RC	
		Newtownbond	14		G
		Shanmullagh	2,5	RC	
16	Mohill				
17	Mostrim	Edgeworthstown, Church Lane	15	EC	G
		Dublin Road		RC	
18	Moydow	Aughine	18,19	RC	
		Moydow Glebe	19	EC	G
19	Noughaval				

NGA No.	CIVIL PARISH	TOWNLAND OR TOWN, STREET	OS No.	CHURCH	GRAVE-YARD
20	Rathcline	Town of Lanesborough	17	RC	
				EC	
21	Rathreagh	Foxhall Glebe	24		G
22	Shrule	Ballymahon, Main Street	27	EC	
				RC	
23	Street	Coolambe	15,16		G
		Lechurragh	15	EC	
24	Taghsheenod	Abbeyderg	18,19, 22,23		G
		Killeendowd	23	RC	
		Taghsheenod Glebe	19,23		G
25	Taghshinny	Taghshinny	23	EC	G
26	Templemichael	Abbeycartron	13	P	
		Cooleeny	14	RC	
		Longford, Chapel Lane	13	RC and new RC unfinish-ed	
		Church Street		M	
				EC	G
		Connaught Street		M	

164

NGA No.	CIVIL PARISH	TOWNLAND OR TOWN, STREET	OS No.	CHURCH	GRAVE-YARD
1	Ardee	Ardee, John Street	14,17	RC	
		Market Street, (East Side)		M	
				EC	G
2	Ballybarrack				
3	Ballyboys	Bellurgan	5,7, 8	RC	
4	Ballymakenny	Ballymakenny	21	EC	G
5	Ballymascanlan	Ballymascanlan	4,7	EC	G
		Doolargy	4,5	RC	
		Faughart Upper	4		G
		Kilcurry	4	RC	
				EC	G
		Piedmont	8	RC	
		Plaster	4	P	
6	Barronstown	Plaster	6	RC	
7	Beaulieu	Beaulieu	25	EC	G
8	Cappoge	Cappoge	18		G
9	Carlingford	Carlingford, Back Lane	5,8	M	
		Church Lane		EC	G
		Dundalk Street (Old Road)		RC	
		Meeting Street		P	
		Castletowncooley	8	RC (Old)	
				RC	
		Drummullagh	2,5	EC	
		Grange Irish	8	RC	
		Knocknagoran	5	RC	
					G
		Mountbagnall	8		G
		Much Grange	9		Part of old G
		Rathcor	8	EC	
10	Carrickbaggot				
11	Castletown	Castletown	7		G

NGA No.	CIVIL PARISH	TOWNLAND OR TOWN, STREET	OS No.	CHURCH	GRAVE- YARD
12	Charlestown	Charlestown	14	EC	G
13	Clogher	Callystown	22	RC	
		Town of Clogher, Main Street	22	EC in Ruins	G
14	Clonkeehan				
15	Clonkeen	Churchtown	13	EC	G
16	Clonmore	Ardballan	18,19	RC	
		Clonmore	18,19	EC	G
17	Collon	Collon, Ardee Street	20	M	
		Chapel Lane		RC	
		Church Street			G
				EC	
18	Creggan	Courtbane	3	RC	
19	Darver	Darver	11,12	EC	G
		Newtowndarver	11,12, 14,15	RC	
20	Dromin	Dromin	18	RC	
				EC	
					G
21	Dromiskin	Dromiskin	12,15	RC	
				EC	G
22	Drumcar	Drumcar	15,18	EC	G
		Willistown	15,18	RC	
23	Drumshallon	Fieldstown	21	RC	
24	Dunany	Dunany	16,19	EC	
25	Dunbin				
26	Dundalk	Dundalk, Anne Street	7	RC	
		Church Street		EC	G
		Jocelyn Street		P	
				M	
		Roden Place		RC	
		Seatown			G
		Seatown Place		RC	
		Wellington Place		M	
27	Dunleer	Dunleer, Main Street	18	RC EC	G

NGA No.	CIVIL PARISH	TOWNLAND OR TOWN, STREET	OS No.	CHURCH	GRAVE-YARD
28	Dysart	Barmeath	18	RC	
		Dysart	18		G
29	Faughart	Dungooly	3,4		G
30	Gernonstown	Castlebellingham	15	EC	
		Town of Castlebellingham	15	P	
31	Haggardstown	Haggardstown	7,12	RC	
					G
32	Haynestown				
33	Inishkeen				
34	Jonesborough				
35	Kane	Kane	3		G
		Killin	4,6, 7	RC	
36	Kildemock	Drakestown	17,20	RC	
					G
		Millockstown	17		G
37	Killanny	Killanny	10	RC	G
38	Killincoole	Killincoole	11	EC	
39	Kilsaran	Kilsaran	15		G
				RC	
40	Louth	Corcreeghagh	10	RC	
		Knockatavy	6,11	RC	
		Town of Louth	11	RC	
		Priorstate	11		G
		Richard Taaffes Holding	11	EC	
		Rootate	10,11	RC	
41	Mansfieldtown	Bawn	14,15	EC	
42	Mappastown	Mapastown	14		Old G
43	Marlestown				
44	Mayne	Glebe East	19,22		G
45	Monasterboice	Monasterboice	21		G
46	Mosstown	Mosstown North	18		G
		Philipstown	17,18	RC	
47	Mullary	Castletown	18,21	EC	G
		Finure	21	RC	

NGA No.	CIVIL PARISH	TOWNLAND OR TOWN, STREET	OS No.	CHURCH	GRAVE-YARD
48	Parsonstown				
49	Philipstown	Philipstown	11		G
		Philipstown	3,6	EC	
		Reaghstown	10,11, 13,14	RC	
50	Port	Port	19		G
51	Rathdrumin	Glebe	18	EC	G
		Walshestown	18,19, 22	RC	
52	Richardstown				
53	Roche				
54	St. Mary's	Drogheda, James Street	24	RC	
		New Road		EC	G
55	St. Peter's	Drogheda, Batchelor's Lane	24	RC	
				ChapelHo. Dwelling	
		Churchyard		St.Peters EC	G
		Cord Lane and Prospect Road		Sienna Convent Chapel	
		Fair Street		St.Marks EC	
				Present-ation Convent	
				Present-ation Convent	
				Site for RC	
		Thomas Street			G
		Linenhall Street East		RC	
		Palace Street		P	
		St. Laurence Street		RC	
				M	
		West Street		RC	
		Killineer	21,24		G

NGA No.	CIVIL PARISH	TOWNLAND OR TOWN, STREET	OS No.	CHURCH	GRAVE-YARD
56	Salterstown	Salterstown	15,16, 19		G
57	Shanlis	Shanlis	17		G
58	Smarmore	Smarmore	17,20		G
59	Stabannan	Stabannan	14,15, 17,18	RC	
				EC	G
60	Stickillin	Stickillin	14,17		G
61	Tallanstown	Louth Hall	11,14	RC	
					G
62	Termonfeckin	Milltown	21,22	RC	
		Town of Termonfeckin	22	RC	
				EC	G
63	Tullyallen	Newtownstalaban	21,24 25		G
				RC	
		Townleyhall	23,24	EC	G
		Tullyallen	21,24	RC	G

NGA No.	CIVIL PARISH	TOWNLAND OR TOWN, STREET	OS No.	CHURCH	GRAVE-YARD
1	Achill	Achill Missionary Settlement, The Square	42	EC	
		Derreen	65	RC	
		Doogort East	42,43	EC	G
		Dookinelly (Calvy)	42,43, 54,55	RC	
		Mweelin	54,55	EC	G
		Pollranny	55,65	EC	G
2	Addergoole	Ballyteige	58,68		G
		Curraghmore	47,52	EC	
		Gortnaheltia	58,68	RC	
		Knockmaria or Addergoole	47		G
		Lahardaun	47	RC	
3	Aghagower	Aghagower	88,98	RC	G
		Derryherbert	107,108	RC	
		Knappaghmore	87,88, 98	EC	
		Lankill	88,98		G
		Srahatloe	116	EC	
		Toberrooaun	88,98	EC	G
4	Aghamore	Aghamore	81,82		G
		Boleyboy	82		G
		Carrowneden	82,92, 93		G
		Cloongawnagh (Cosgrave)	82		G
		Killeen	81	RC	
5	Aglish	Ballynew	69,70, 78		G
		Castlebar, Church Street	78	EC	G
		The Green or Mall		M	
		Rock Square		Convent Chapel	
		Upper Chapel Street		RC	
		Knockacroghery	78		G
6	Annagh	Coolnafarna	93,103		G

NGA No.	CIVIL PARISH	TOWNLAND OR TOWN, STREET	OS No.	CHURCH	GRAVE- YARD
6	Annagh	Friarsground	93	RC	G
		Hazelhill	93,103	RC	
		Kildarra	102		G
		Lugboy Demesne	103	RC	
7	Ardagh	Carrowcrin	30	RC	
8	Attymass	Bunnafinglas	48		G
		Kilgellia	40,49	RC	
9	Balla	Town of Balla	90	RC	G
10	Ballinchalla	Ballinchalla	117		G
11	Ballinrobe	Ballinrobe, Chapel Road Market Street	110,118	RC RC in Progress EC	
		Carrownalecka	110,118		G
		Cornaroya	118	RC	
		Friarsquarter West	118		G
12	Ballintober	Ballintober	89,99		G
		Bellaburk	89		G
		Kilbree Upper	88		G
		Killavally West	89,99	RC	
13	Ballyhean	Cloonaghmore	89	RC	
		Cunnaker	89	EC	
		Errew	89	EC	
14	Ballynahaglish	Ballynahaglish	39		G
		Knockmore	48	RC	
15	Ballyovey	Cappaghduff East	109,117	EC	
		Gorteenmore	109	RC	G
		Kilkeeran	99,109, 110		G
		Knockleanore	109	RC	
		Treanlaur	109	RC	
16	Ballysakeery	Ballysakeery	22		G
		Cloonshinnagh	22	M	

NGA No.	CIVIL PARISH	TOWNLAND OR TOWN, STREET	OS No.	CHURCH	GRAVE-YARD
16	Ballysakeery	Coonealmore	22	RC	
		Lisglennon	22	EC	
		Mullaferry	22	P	
17	Bekan	Bekan	92,102	RC	G
18	Bohola	Toocananagh	71,81	RC	
19	Breaghwy	Breaghwy	79	RC	
		Demesne	79		G
20	Burriscarra	Carrownacon	100	RC	
		Castlecarra	100		G
21	Burrishoole	Carrowkeel	67		G
		Newfield	67	RC	
		Newport, Barrack Hill	67,68	RC	
		Church Lane		EC	G
	Castlemore	Glebe	74		G
22	Cong	Cong South (Detached portion)	120	EC	
		Cong South	120	EC in ruins RC	G
		Lecarrowkilleen	121	EC	G
23	Crossboyne	Ballindine North	111,112	RC	
		Ballyglass	111,119	RC	
		Burris	111	RC	
		Crossboyne	111	EC	G
24	Crossmolina	Crossmolina	38	EC	G
		Town of Crossmolina	29,38	M RC	
		Keenagh Beg	37,46	RC	
		Kilmurry More	38	RC	G
25	Doonfeeny	Ballinglen	7,13, 14	P	
		Ballycastle, Main Street	7,14	EC	G
		Beldergmore	5,6	RC	
		Carrowkibbock Upper	7,14	RC	
26	Drum	Cuillare	90	RC RC in progress	

NGA No.	CIVIL PARISH	TOWNLAND OR TOWN, STREET	OS No.	CHURCH	GRAVE-YARD
26	Drum	Drum or Knockatemple	90		G
		Elmhall	79,90		G
		Glebe	90	EC	
		Gweeshadan	90		G
	Inishbofin	Middlequarter	114	RC	
27	Islandeady	Barnastang	68,69	RC	
		Cloonan	77,78	RC	
		Drumneen	77,88		G
		Islandeady	78		G
28	Kilbeagh	Cashelduff	63,73	RC	G
		Cloonfane	63		G
		Killeen	62		G
		Srah Lower	51,63		G
		Temple	63	RC	G
		Tonnagh	51,63		G
29	Kilbelfad	Glebe	39		G
30	Kilbride				
31	Kilcolman	Ballaghaderreen, Chapel Lane Pound Street	74	RC EC RC in progress	G
		Ballyoughter	74		G
		Claremorris, Chapel Lane Church Street	101	RC EC	
		Creggan	64,74, 83	RC	G
		Hawksford	64		G
		Mace Upper	91,92	RC	
32	Kilcommon	Aghoos	11	RC	
		Ballybeg	26	RC in progress	
		Bangor	18,26	EC	
		Belmullet	10	RC	

NGA No.	CIVIL PARISH	TOWNLAND OR TOWN, STREET	OS No.	CHURCH	GRAVE-YARD
32	Kilcommon	Belmullet, Ballyglass Street	10,17	M	
		Bridge Street		RC	
		Bunnahowen	17	RC	G
		Carrowmore	119	RC	
		Castlehill	44	EC	
		Curraunboy	4	RC	
		Fahy	34,43		G
		Hollymount Demesne	110,111	EC	G
		Town of Hollymount	110,111	P	
		Kilcommon or Pollatomish	11	EC	G
		Kilcommon	119		G
		Kilteany	26		G
		Rahard	111,118, 119	RC	
		Rosdoagh	4,11	M	
		Tallagh	43,44	RC	
33	Kilconduff	Rathscanlan	62		G
		Swineford, Chapel Street	62	RC	
				EC	G
34	Kilcummin				
35	Kildacommoge	Ara	79,80		G
		Ballycommon	70	RC	
		Knocktemple	70,71		G
		Moyhenna	70,79		G
36	Kilfian	Kincon	14,21	RC	
37	Kilgarvan	Bunnyconnellan West	31,40	RC	
		Kilgarvan	40		G
38	Kilgeever	Devlin South	105	RC	
		Kilgeever	86,96		G
		Lecarrow	75,81 85	RC	G
		Louisburgh, Bridge Street	86	EC	G
		Chapel Street		RC	
		Roonah	95,96	EC	

NGA No.	CIVIL PARISH	TOWNLAND OR TOWN, STREET	OS No.	CHURCH	GRAVE-YARD
39	Killala	Abbeylands	22		G
		Crosspatrick	22		G
		Killala, Chapel Lane	15,22	RC	
		Church Street		EC	G
		Preaching House Street		M	
40	Killasser	Callow	49,61	RC	
		Coolagagh	49		G
		Graffy	49,61		G
		Knockmullan	49,50		G
		Listernan	61,62	RC	
41	Killeden	Ballinamore	80,91	EC	G
		Town of Kiltamagh	80	RC	
		Oxford	80		G
42	Kilmaclasser	Fahy More	77	RC	
		Rushbrook	77		G
43	Kilmainebeg	Kilkeeran	121		G
		Village of Kilmaine	118,121	EC	G
				Old Abbey	G
44	Kilmainemore	Frenchbrook North	121	RC	
45	Kilmeena	Buckfield	76	EC	
		Islands in Clew Bay	76		G
		Kilmeena	77		G
		Moyna	76	RC	
		Rusheen	76,87		G
46	Kilmolara	Carrownakilly	118		G
		Village of the Neale	118,121	RC	
47	Kilmore	Village of Binghamstown	7,9,16	RC	
		Binghamstown	7,9,16	EC	G
		Cross (Boyd)	16		G
		Fallmore	24,33		G
		Islands	16,23, 33,47		G
		Moyrahan	10		G
		Termoncarragh	9		G

NGA No.	CIVIL PARISH	TOWNLAND OR TOWN, STREET	OS No.	CHURCH	GRAVE-YARD
47	Kilmore	Tiraun	24	RC	
48	Kilmoremoy	Ardoughan	30		G
		Ballina, Charles Street	30	P	
		John Street		BAP	
		Lower Piper Hill		M	
49	Kilmovee	Glentauraun	72,73	RC	
		Kilkelly	72,81		G
		Kilmovee	73	RC	
		Magheraboy	73,74, 83		G
		Rusheens West	73		G
50	Kilturra	Ballindoo or Doocastle	51,52		G
51	Kilvine	Ballinvilla	112	RC	
		Kilvine	112,113		G
52	Knock	Caldragh	92		G
		Churchfield	92	Ruins	G
		Drum	92	RC	
53	Lackan	Castlelackan Demesne	7,8, 14,15	RC	
		Glebe	7,14		G
		Killogeary	14,15	EC	G
54	Manulla	Creaghanboy	79		G
		Rinnahulty	79		G
55	Mayo	Gortaphuntaun	90,101	EC	
		Mayo Parks	90,91	RC	
56	Meelick	Killeen	61,71	RC	
		Meelick	71		G
57	Moorgagagh				
58	Moygawnagh	Ardvarney	21,29	RC	
59	Oughaval	Cahernamart	88	RC	
		Carrowbaun	88		Workhouse G
		Carrowkeel	87		G
		Churchfield	87		G
		Drummin East	97,107	RC	G

NGA No.	CIVIL PARISH	TOWNLAND OR TOWN, STREET	OS No.	CHURCH	GRAVE-YARD
59	Oughaval	Glasspatrick	87		G
		Thornhill	87	RC	
		Westport Demesne	76,77, 87,88	EC	
		Town of Westport,South Mall	88	RC M	
60	Rathreagh				
61	Robeen	Cashel	110	RC	
		Robeen	110		G
62	Rosslee	Rathnacreeva	90		G
63	Shrule	Cloghmoyne	123	RC	
		Mounthenry	123	RC	
		Moyne	123		G
		Ramolin	121,122	RC	
		Shrule	122		G
64	Tagheen	Carrowkeel	101,111	RC	
		Tagheen East	111		G
65	Templemore	Knockagarraun	60,70		G
		Strade	70	RC	G
66	Templemurry				
67	Toomore	Foxford, Chapel Street	48,49 60,61	RC	
		Pound Street		EC	G
		Toomore	61		G
68	Touaghty				
69	Turlought	Crumlin	59,60, 69,70	RC	
		Drumdaff	70	EC	
		Park	70	RC	
		Turlough	70	P M	G

NGA No.	CIVIL PARISH	TOWNLAND OR TOWN, STREET	OS No.	CHURCH	GRAVE-YARD
1	Agher	Agher	42,43, 48,49	EC RC	G
2	Ardagh	Ardagh	2,3	EC	
		Meath Hill	3	RC	
3	Ardbraccan	Ardbraccan	24,25	EC	
		Boyerstown	24,25, 31	RC	
		Neillstown	24	RC	
4	Ardcath	Ardcath	33	RC	G
5	Ardmulchan	Ardmulchan	25,26		G
6	Ardsallagh	Ardsallagh	31		G
7	Assey	Assey	31		G
8	Athboy	Athboy, Chapel Street	29	RC	
		Church Lane		EC	G
9	Athlumney	Athlumney	25		G
		Johnstown	25	RC	
10	Balfeaghan	Balfeaghan	49		G
11	Ballyboggan	Ballyboggan	46,47		G
12	Ballygarth				
13	Ballymagarvey	Ballymagarvey	32		G
14	Ballymaglassan	Ballymaglassan	44,50	EC	G
15	Balrathboyne	Athgaine Great	17,24	EC	
		Betaghstown	24	RC	
		Cortown	17,24		G
16	Balsoon	Balsoon	34		G
17	Bective	Balbradagh	31	RC	
		Bective	31		G
		Gillstown	31	EC	
18	Brownstown	Brownstown	26,32		G
19	Burry	Balrath Demesne	16		G
20	Castlejordan	Baltigeer	46		G
		Castlejordan	52	EC	G

NGA No.	CIVIL PARISH	TOWNLAND OR TOWN, STREET	OS No.	CHURCH	GRAVE-YARD
20	Castlejordan	Kilkeeran	46		G
		Lewellensland	46,52	RC	
		Toor	46	RC	
21	Castlekeeran or Loughan	Castlekeeran	10,16		G
		Loughan	10		G
		Meenlagh	10,16	RC	
22	Castlerickard	Castlerickard	41,42	EC	G
23	Castletown	Castletown	11,12	EC	G
24	Churchtown	Churchtown	30,31		G
		Dunderry	30	RC	
25	Clonalvy	Flemingtown	33		G
				RC	
26	Clonard	Anneville or Clonard(old)	41,47	EC	G
		Croboy	40,41		G
		Hardwood	40,46		G
		Village of Longwood, Longwood Street	41,47	RC	
		Middleborough	47		G
		Ticroghan	46,47		G
		Towlaght	46,47	RC	G
27	Clongill	Clongill	11,17,18		Old G
		Dowthstown	18	RC	
28	Clonmacduff	Meadstown	30		G
29	Collon				
30	Colp	Colp West	20,21	EC	G
		Village of Mornington	21	RC	G
		Stagreenan	20		G
31	Cookstown				
32	Crickstown	Crickstown	38,39	RC	
					G
33	Cruicetown	Cruicetown	5,11		G
				RC	
34	Culmullin	Culmullin	43,44		G
				RC	

NGA No.	CIVIL PARISH	TOWNLAND OR TOWN, STREET	OS No.	CHURCH	GRAVE-YARD
35	Cushinstown	Roadmain	33		G
36	Danestown	Danestown	32		G
37	Derrypatrick	Derrypatrick	37,43		G
38	Diamor	Bobsville	15		G
39	Donaghmore	Donaghmore	25		G
		Donaghmore	45	RC	G
40	Donaghpatrick	Gibstown Demesne	17,18	EC	
41	Donove	Cruicerath	20,27	RC	
42	Dowdstown				
43	Dowth	Dowth	19,20		G
44	Drakestown	Drakestown	11,12		G
		Leggagh	12	RC	
45	Drumcondra	Drumbride	3		G
		Drumcondra	6	EC	G
		Rathtrasna	3,6	RC	
46	Drumlargan				
47	Dulane	Dulane	11,17		G
48	Duleek	Collierstown	27	RC	
		Duleek, Church Lane	27	EC	G
		Main Street		RC	
		Roughgrange	19,20, 26,27		G
49	Duleek Abbey				
50	Dunboyne	Town of Dunboyne	50	RC	
				EC	
		Loughsallagh	50,51		G
51	Dunmoe	Dunmoe	18,25		G
52	Dunsany	Dunsany	37,38	RC	
53	Dunshauglin	Dunshauglin, Drogheda Road	38,44	EC	G
		Main Street		RC	
54	Emlagh				
55	Enniskeen	Ervey	2	P	
56	Fennor	Fennor	19		G
57	Follistown	Follistown	25,26, 31,32		G

NGA No.	CIVIL PARISH	TOWNLAND OR TOWN, STREET	OS No.	CHURCH	GRAVE-YARD
58	Gallow	Gallow	49		G
59	Galtrim	Boycetown	37,43	RC	
		Galtrim	37,43	EC	
60	Gernonstown	Gernonstown	18,19		G
61	Girley	Girley	23		G
				RC	
62	Grangegeeth	Grangegeeth	13,19	RC	
					G
63	Greenoge				
64	Inishmot				
65	Julianstown	Dimanistown West	28	RC	
		Julianstown West	21,28	EC	G
66	Kells	Cakestown Glebe	17	RC	
		Commons of Lloyd	16,17		G
		Kells, Church Street	16,17	EC	
		Headfort Place		RC	
					G
67	Kentstown	Kentstown	26,32	RC	
				EC	
68	Kilbeg	Kilbeg Upper	11		G
		Robertstown	5,11		G
		Thomastown	11	RC	
69	Kilberry	Kilberry	18	RC	
					G
70	Kilbrew	Kilbrew	38,39	EC	G
71	Kilbride	Baytown	45,51		G
		Priesttown	45,51	RC	
72	Kilcarn	Kilcarn	25,31		G
73	Kilclone	Kilclone	49,50		G
		Mulhussey	49		G
		Pagestown	49,50	RC	
74	Kilcooly	Kiltoome	36		G
75	Kildalkey	Kildalkey	29,30, 35,36		G

NGA No.	CIVIL PARISH	TOWNLAND OR TOWN, STREET	OS No.	CHURCH	GRAVE-YARD
75	Kildalkey	Village of Kildalkey	29,30, 35,36	RC	
		Moyrath	29,35, 36	EC	
76	Killaconnigan	Village of Ballivor	35	EC	
		Kilballivor	35	RC	
		Killaconnigan	35		G
77	Killallon	Boherhard	22		G
		Killacroy	22	RC	
78	Killary	Heronstown	12	RC	
		Killary	12	RC	G
79	Killeagh	Church Island	8		G
		Moat	8	EC RC	G
80	Killeen				
81	Killegland	Ashbourne, Main Street	39,45	RC	
		Killegland	39,45	G	
82	Killyon	Boraheen	41	RC	
		Clondaleemore	35,41		G
		Killyon	41		G
83	Kilmainham	Village of Kilmainham	5	RC	
		Kilmainham Wood	2,5	EC	G
84	Kilmessan	Kilmessan	37	RC EC	
85	Kilmoon	Kilmoon	32,33, 38	EC	G
86	Kilmore	Arodstown	43		G
		Kilmore	43,49	EC	G
		Moynalvy	43	RC	
87	Kilsharvan	Kilsharvan	27		G
88	Kilshine	Knightstown	12,18	EC	G
89	Kilskeer	Crossakeel	16	EC	
		Kilskeer	16,23	RC	G

COUNTY MEATH

NGA No.	CIVIL PARISH	TOWNLAND OR TOWN, STREET	OS No.	CHURCH	GRAVE-YARD
89	Kilskeer	Smithstown	16,23	RC	
90	Kiltale				
91	Knock				
92	Knockcommon	Knockcommon	26		G
		Rossnaree	1,9, 26	RC	
93	Knockmark	Knockmark	38,43, 44	EC	G
94	Laracor	Dangan	42,43	RC	
		Laracor	36,42	EC	
		Town of Summerhill	42,43	P	
		Summerhill Demesne	42,43		G
95	Liscartan				
96	Lismullin	Lismullin	31,32	EC	G
97	Loughbrackan				
98	Loughcrew	Loughcrew	15	Old EC	G
		Rahaghy	15	EC	
99	Macetown				
100	Martry	Allenstown Demesne	24		G
101	Mitchelstown				
102	Monknewtown	Monknewtown	19	RC	G
103	Monktown	Monktown	26,32		G
		Walterstown	32	RC	
104	Moorechurch	Moorechurch	28		G
		Sarsfieldstown	28	RC	
105	Moybolgne	Corgreagh or Killagriff	1,2	EC	
		Mullaghavally	2,5		G
		Teevurcher	1	RC	
106	Moyglare	Moyglare	49,50	EC	G
107	Moylagh	Garrymabolie	15	RC	
		Moylagh	14,15		G
108	Moymet	Kilbride	30	RC	
		Moymet	30		G
109	Moynalty	Moynalty	10,11	RC	

183

NGA No.	CIVIL PARISH	TOWNLAND OR TOWN, STREET	OS No.	CHURCH	GRAVE-YARD
109	Moynalty	Village of Moynalty	10,11	EC	G
		Newcastle	4	RC	
110	Navan	Navan, Academy Street	25	RC	
		Chapel Lane		RC	
		Church Hill		EC	G
		Trimgate Street		RC	
111	Newtown	Newtown	11	EC	
112	Newtownclonkun	Village of Newtowntrim	36		G
113	Nobber	Nobber	5,6	RC	
				EC	G
114	Oldcastle	Oldcastle	9		G
		Oldcastle, Chapel Street	9	RC	
				M	
		Market Square		EC	G
115	Painestown	Painestown	19,26	EC	
		Seneschalstown	26	RC	
116	Piercetown	Piercetown	33		G
117	Rataine	Rataine	30,31		G
118	Rathbeggan	Rathbeggan	44	EC	G
119	Rathcore	Kilcorney	48	RC	
		Rathcore	42,48	EC	
120	Rathfeigh	Rathfeigh	32	RC	
					G
121	Rathkenny	Rathkenny	12,18	RC	
				EC	G
122	Rathmolyon	Ardanew	42		Old G
		Kilballyporter	42	RC	
		Village of Rathmolyon	42	EC	
123	Rathmore	Moyagher Lower	24		G
		Rathmore	24,30	RC	G
124	Rathregan	Rathregan	44	RC	
					G
125	Ratoath	Ratoath, Main Street	45	RC	
				EC	G

NGA No.	CIVIL PARISH	TOWNLAND OR TOWN, STREET	OS No.	CHURCH	GRAVE-YARD
126	Rodanstown	Newtownmoyaghy	49	RC	
		Rodanstown	49	EC	G
127	St Mary's				
128	Scurlockstown	Scurlockstown	36,37		G
129	Siddan	Creevagh	6,7	RC	
		Siddan	6	EC	G
130	Skreen	Collierstown	32,38	RC	
		Skreen	32		G
131	Slane	Rushwee	18,19	RC	
		Town of Slane	19	RC	
				EC	
		Slane Castle Demesne	19		G
132	Stackallan	Stackallan	18,19, 25,26	EC	
133	Staffordstown				
134	Staholmog	Staholmog	11	RC	
					G
135	Stamullin	Village of Stamullin	28,34	RC	
					G
136	Tara	Castleboy	31,37	EC	G
137	Teltown	Oristown	11,17		G
				RC	
		Teltown	17		G
138	Templekeeran				
139	Timoole	Timoole	32,33		G
140	Trevet	Trevet	38		G
141	Trim	Brannockstown	36,42	RC	
					G
		Derrinydaly	36		G
		Friaryland	36		G
		Glebe	41		G
		Trim, Chapel Street	36	RC	
		Church Street		EC	G
		Main Street		M	
		Tremblestown	36	RC	G

185

NGA No.	CIVIL PARISH	TOWNLAND OR TOWN, STREET	OS No.	CHURCH	GRAVE-YARD
142	Trubley				
143	Tullaghanoge				
144	Tullyallen				

NGA No.	CIVIL PARISH	TOWNLAND OR TOWN, STREET	OS No.	CHURCH	GRAVE-YARD
1	Aghabog	Aghadrumkeen	18	P	
		Crover	17	EC	G
		Drumshannon	17	P	G
		Latnamard	13	RC	G
2	Aghnamullen	Aghmakerr	24	RC	G
		Annahaia	24	RC	
		Corlat	27		G
		Corlea	24,27	P	G
		Corvackan	26	EC	
		Creeve	24	P	
		Crossduff	24,27	EC	G
		Drumcunnion	26,27	RC	G
		Lattonfasky	24		G
		Lisdrumcleve	23	RC	G
		Moyle More	23	EC	
		Tullyrain	27	RC	
		Ullinagh	24	P	
3	Ballybay	Ballybay, Monaghan Road	19	RC	
		Cornamucklaglass	19	EC	
				RC	
		Derrynaloobinagh	19	P	
		Derryvally	18,19	P	
		Tonyglassan	19	RC	
4	Clones	Clones, Abbey Lane	11		G
		Cara Street		M	
		The Diamond		EC	G
		Monaghan Street		P	
		Whitehall Street		M	G
		Clontibret	11,12, 16,17		G
		Gransha More	12	P	
		Largy	12	RC	
		Selloo	8	M	
		Town of Smithborough	12	P	
		Templetate	12	RC	G

COUNTY MONAGHAN

NGA No.	CIVIL PARISH	TOWNLAND OR TOWN, STREET	OS No.	CHURCH	GRAVE-YARD
5	Clontibret	Annayalla	14,19	RC	G
		Doohamlat	19	RC	
		Gallagh	14	EC	G
		Tullybuck	14	RC	
6	Currin	Aghnahola	16	EC	G
		Corrinshigo	22	RC	
		Cortober	22	EC	
				P	G
		Drum	22	P	G
		Killyfargy	16		G
		Lisnalee	16	RC	
7	Donagh	Carrigans	6	P	
		Cloncaw	7	RC	
		Derryhallagh	6	RC	G
		Donagh	6,7		G
		Town of Emyvale	6	M	
		Glaslough	7	EC	G
		Town of Glaslough	7	M	
		Letloonigan	7	P	G
		Mullabrack (Scott)	6,9	SP	
		Mullamurphy	9	RC	
8	Donaghmoyne	Brackagh	25	P	
				EC	
		Donaghmoyne	28,31	EC	G
		Drumcattan	28,29	RC	G
		Lisdoonan	28	RC	G
		Taplagh	25,28	RC	G
		Tullymackilmartin	28	RC	
9	Drummully	Cloonoony	16	EC	G
		Clontask	16	RC	G
10	Drumsnat	Drumguill	13	RC	
		Mullanacross	9,12, 13		G
				EC	G
11	Ematris	Carsan	22,23	RC	

COUNTY MONAGHAN

NGA No.	CIVIL PARISH	TOWNLAND OR TOWN, STREET	OS No.	CHURCH	GRAVE-YARD
11	Ematris	Corravacan	18	RC	
		Dawson Grove Demesne	22,23	EC	G
		Edergole	18		G
		Town of Rockcorry	18,23	P	
				EC	G
				M	
				M	
12	Errigal Trough	Drumbristan	3	RC	G
		Knockconan	3	RC	G
		Mullanacross	3		G
		Mullanderg	3	EC	G
		Shanco	3	EC	
		Tavanagh	1,3	RC	
13	Inishkeen	Inishkeen Glebe	29	EC	G
		Lacklom	29,32	RC	G
14	Killanny	Aghafad	31	EC	G
15	Killeevan	Aghnamard	17	RC	
		Drumswords	17		G
		Killeevan Glebe	12	EC	
			17		G
		Killyfuddy	12	RC	G
		Newbliss	17	EC	
		Shanco	12	Old Church	G
					G
16	Kilmore	Corcaghan	13	RC	G
		Kilnahaltar	9	EC	G
		Slieveroe	13,18		G
17	Magheracloone	Camaghy	30,33	EC	G
		Carrickashedoge	34	RC	
		Knocknacran East	30,31,34	RC	
					G
		Mullaghgarve	34	EC	
18	Magheross	Carrickmaclim	30,31		G

COUNTY MONAGHAN

NGA No.	CIVIL PARISH	TOWNLAND OR TOWN, STREET	OS No.	CHURCH	GRAVE-YARD
18	Magheross	Town of Carrickmacross	31		G
		Carrickmacross, Main Street		EC	G
		New Street		RC	
		Cloghvally	31		G
		Corduff	27	RC	
		Corgreeghagh	27,30	RC	
		Shanco	27,30	P	
19	Monaghan	Aghananimy	9	RC	G
		Legnacreeve	14		G
				P	
		Lisleitrim	14	RC	
		Monaghan, Church Square	9	M	
				EC	G
		Dawson Street		M	
		Market Street		M	
		Meeting House Square		P	G
		Park Street		RC	
		Rackwallace	14		G
		Tirkeenan	9		G
20	Muckno	Aghnadanph	20	P	
		Annyart	20	SP	
		Castleblaney, Church Street	20,25	M	
		Church Hill	20		G
		Drumillard Big	20,25	P	
		Formil	20	P	G
		Loughbrattoge	15	P	G
		Onomy	20,25	EC	G
				RC	G
		Oram	20	RC	G
21	Tedavnet	Bough	8,9	P	G
		Derrynagrew	9	SP	G
		Drumdesco	6,9	RC	G

NGA No.	CIVIL PARISH	TOWNLAND OR TOWN, STREET	OS No.	CHURCH	GRAVE-YARD
21	Tedavnet	Mullaghmore West	9	EC	G
		Mullanarockan	6		G
		Village of Tedavnet	6	RC	
22	Tehallan	Leitrim	10	RC	
		Templetate	10	EC	G
23	Tullycorbet	Corlea	13,14	P	G
		Corvoy	19	RC	G
		Creevagh	18,19	COV	G
		Lisnaveane	18	P	G
		Terrygeely	14	EC	G

NGA No.	CIVIL PARISH	TOWNLAND OR TOWN, STREET	OS No.	CHURCH	GRAVE-YARD
1	Aghancon	Ballybritt	43	RC	
		Glebe	39	EC	
2	Ardnurcher or Horseleap				
3	Ballyboy	Ballyboy	31	EC	
		Frankford, Chapel Lane (off Main Street)	31	RC	
		Kinnetty Road	31	M	
4	Ballyburly	Ballyburly	4,11	EC	
		Road	11	RC	
5	Ballycommon	Ballycommon	18	EC	G
		Ballyteige Little	17	RC	G
6	Ballykean	Ballinvoker	26	RC	G
		Ballykean	26		G
		Stranure	26	EC	G
		Urney	26		G
7	Ballymacwilliam				
8	Ballynakill	Ballynakill	11,19		G
9	Birr	Birr, Castle Street	35	CY	
		Church Lane		Old EC in ruins	G
		Cumberland Street		EC	
				BAP	
				M	
		Graveyard Street			Quaker G
		Main Street		Q	
		Oxmantown Mall		Convent RC	
		Drumbane	35		G
10	Borrisnafarney	Ballycormick	46	EC	G
11	Castlefordan				
12	Castletownely	Drumroe	47		G
13	Clonmacnoise	Clonfinlough	6	RC	
		Clonmacnoise	5,6	EC	
		Glebe	6		G
		Town of Shannonbridge	13	RC	

NGA No.	CIVIL PARISH	TOWNLAND OR TOWN, STREET	OS No.	CHURCH	GRAVE-YARD
14	Clonsast	Bracknagh	27,28	RC	
					G
		Clonbulloge	19,20	EC	G
				RC	
		Cloncreen	19		G
		Clonsast Upper	28		G
		Coolygagan	20,28		G
15	Clonyhurk	Clonyhurk	33		G
		Garryhinch	33	EC	G
		Portarlington, Main Street	34	M	
				RC	
16	Corbally				
17	Croghan	Croghan Demesne	10	RC	G
		Croghan Hill	10		G
18	Cullenwaine	Cullenwaine	44,46		G
		Moneygall	46,47	RC	
19	Drumcullen	Rathmount	30,31	RC	
20	Dunkerrin	Barna	44,45	RC	
		Franckfort	45	EC	G
				RC	
21	Durrow	Ballybought	8,9	RC	G
		Durrow Demesne	8,9	EC	G
22	Eglish	Ballycollin	30	RC	G
		Dovegrove	35		G
		Eglish	30	EC	G
23	Ettagh	Ballyknockan	42	RC	
		Glebe	42	EC	G
24	Finglass	Loughan	45,47		G
25	Gallen	Town of Cloghan	22	RC	
				EC	
		Gallen	14,22		G
		Kilcamin	22		G
		Killowneybeg	22		G
26	Geashill	Ballingar	18	RC	

NGA No.	CIVIL PARISH	TOWNLAND OR TOWN, STREET	OS No.	CHURCH	GRAVE-YARD
26	Geashill	Ballymooney	18		G
		Coolagarry	27	RC	
		Village of Geashill	26	EC	
		Gorteen	25	M	
		Killeigh	25	RC	
		Village of Killeigh	25	RC	
27	Kilbride	Town of Clara	8	RC	
		Clara, East Fair Green Street	8	EC	G
		Clonminch	17		G
		Erry Armstrong	8		G
		Kilbride	16		G
		Kilcoursey	8		G
		Kilcruttin	17		G
		Lehinch	8	RC	G
		Lissanisky	2,8		G
		Tullamore	17	EC	
		Town of Tullamore	17		G
		Tullamore, Bury Quay		Convent	
		Charles Street	17	RC	
		Charleville Square		EC	
		Church Street		M	
		Crowe Street		M	
		Earl Street		Q	
28	Kilclonfert	Cloncarrow or River Lyons	18		G
		Clyduff	10	RC	G
		Kilclonfert	10		G
29	Kilcolman	Ballygaddy	38	RC	
		Cree	38	EC	
		Kilcolman	38		G
30	Kilcomin	Kilcomin	41		G
31	Kilcumreragh				
32	Killaderry	Killaderry	10		G
		Philipstown, Main Street	10,18	EC	G
				M	

194

NGA No.	CIVIL PARISH	TOWNLAND OR TOWN, STREET	OS No.	CHURCH	GRAVE-YARD
32	Killaderry	Philipstown, Chapel Lane	10,18	RC	
				M	
33	Wheery	Ferbane, Ballycumber Road	14	M	
		Chapel Lane or Moystown Road		RC	
		Main Street		EC	G
		Kincora	15		G
34	Killoughy	Annaghbrack Glebe	32		G
		Gortacur	24,32	RC	G
		Mountpleasant	24	EC	G
		Rathlihen	21		G
35	Kilmanaghan	Kilmanaghan	2,8		G
		Tober	1,2	RC	
36	Kilmurrayely	Brosna	42	RC	
37	Kinnitty	Clonlee	36,39	RC	
		Kinnitty	36	RC	
				EC	G
38	Lemanaghan	Grogan and Corroe	7	EC	G
		Parkaree or Boherfadda	7	RC	
39	Letterluna	Codamstown	31,32, 36,37	RC	
40	Lusmagh	Gortareven	29	RC	
41	Lynally	Lynally Glebe	16		G
				EC	G
		Mucklagh	16,24	RC	G
42	Monasteroris	Drumcooly	11,12		G
		Edenderry	12	RC	
					Quaker G
		Edenderry, Church Walk	12	EC	G
		Coney Burrow Street Upper		Q	
		Market Square		M	
		Monasteroris	11,12		G
		Shean	12,20		G
43	Rahan	Churchhill	16		G

NGA No.	CIVIL PARISH	TOWNLAND OR TOWN, STREET	OS No.	CHURCH	GRAVE-YARD
43	Rahan	Killina	16	RC	
		Kilpatrick	7,8 16	RC	
		Rahan Demesne	16	EC	G
		Tullybeg	16	RC	
44	Roynagh	Banagher, Church Lane or Green Street	21,29	EC in ruins	G
		Main Street	21,29	RC	
		Feeghs	29,30	EC	G
		Garrycastle	29,30		G
45	Roscomroe	Gorteen	43	RC	
		Roscomroe	39		G
46	Roscrea	Ballybrack	45		G
47	Seirkieran	Aghagurty	39		G
		Breaghmore	36	RC	
		Churchland	36,39	EC	G
		Fancroft	43		G
				RC	
48	Shinrone	Town of Shinrone	42	RC	
				M	
				M	
49	Templeharry	Ballintemple	44	EC	G
		Graffan	44		G
50	Tisaran	Deerpark	14	EC	G
		Farranmackshane	14	RC	
		Moystown Demesne	22		G

COUNTY ROSCOMMON

NGA No.	CIVIL PARISH	TOWNLAND OR TOWN, STREET	OS No.	CHURCH	GRAVE-YARD
1	Ardcarn	Ardcarn	6	EC	G
		Crossna	3	RC	
		Demesne	6	EC	
		Knockadaff	6		G
2	Athleague	Athleague, Main Street	41	RC	
		Glebe	41	EC	G
3	Aughrim	Ardlougher	17	EC	G
		Aughrim	17		G
		Lisnanuran	11,17	RC	
		Rodeen	17	RC	
	Ballintemple	Cloonfinlough	29		G
4	Ballintober	Ballintober	27	RC	G
5	Ballynakill				
6	Baslick	Baslick	21		G
		Kilmurry	21,27		G
		Pollranny	27	RC	
		Toberelva	27		G
7	Boyle	Aghacarra	3	RC	
		Boyle, Chapel Lane	6	RC	
		Sligo Road		EC	
				M	
		Knocknashee	6	EC	G
		Termon	5,6	M	
8	Bumlin	Bumlin	29		G
		Scramoge	29	RC	
		Strokestown, Church Street	23,29	EC	
		Elphin Street		RC	
9	Cam	Cam	48		G
		Carrick	45,48		G
				RC	
10	Castlemore				
11	Clooncraff	Clooncraff	17		G
		Kye	17	RC	
		Lecarrow	17,18	RC	

197

NGA No.	CIVIL PARISH	TOWNLAND OR TOWN, STREET	OS No.	CHURCH	GRAVE-YARD
12	Cloonfinlough	Carrownaskeagh	29	RC	
13	Cloontuskert	Ballyleague	37	RC in Progress	
		Cloontuskert	36,37		G
14	Cloonygormican	Ballymacurly South	55	RC	
		Carrowbaun	28	EC	G
		Clogher	35		G
15	Creagh	Creagh	53	RC	
		Kilgarve	53		G
16	Creeve	Creeve	17		G
		Lecarrow	10,11 16	EC	
		Ryefield or Runnateggal	16	RC	
17	Drum	Curryroe	51	RC	G
		Thomastown Demesne	51,54		G
18	Drumatemple				
	Drumercool	Killukin	11	RC	
19	Dunamon				
20	Dysart				
21	Elphin	Elphin, Main Street	16	P	
		Killynaghmore	22		G
		Lisnagard	22	RC	
22	Estersnow	Carrowkeel	10	EC	
		Estersnow	10	EC	G
23	Fuerty	Village of Fuerty	39	EC	
		Creemully and Aghagad Beg	38,39 41	RC	
		Lisgallan	35,39	RC	
24	Kilbride	Ballinderry	35,36	RC	
		Grange	28,35		G
25	Kilbryan	Annagh or Drumanilra	3	EC	
26	Kilcolagh	Knockglass	9,10, 15	RC	
27	Kilcolman				
28	Kilcooley	Kilcooley	28		G
29	Kilcorkey	Village of Bellanagare	15,21	RC	
		Mountdruid	21		G

NGA No.	CIVIL PARISH	TOWNLAND OR TOWN, STREET	OS No.	CHURCH	GRAVE-YARD
30	Kilgefin	Ballagh	36	RC	
		Cartron or Old Glebe	36	EC	G
31	Kilglass	Ballymoylin	24		G
		Clooneen (Hartland)	23		G
		Glebe	23,24		G
		Kilgarve	18	RC	
		Legan	23,24	RC	
		Moher	24	RC	
		Moyglass	23	RC	
		Rooaun	23,24	EC	
32	Kilkeevin	Arm	26	RC	G
		Castlereagh, Main Street	26	M	
		Cloocan	19		G
		Demesne	20,26		G
		Knockroe	26	EC	G
33	Killinvoy	Glebe	42	EC	
		Killeenrevagh	42	RC	
34	Killukin	Village of Croghan	10	RC	
		Killukin	11	EC	G
		Lodge	11	RC	
35	Killummod	Killummod	11		G
		Knockroe	10,16		G
36	Kilmacumsy	Caldragh	16		G
37	Kilmeane	Corgrave	42	Q	
		Corroy	42	RC	
		Mote Demesne	41,42		G
		Portrunny	42		G
38	Kilmore	Dungan (King)	11,17	RC	
		Kilmore	12,18	EC	G
39	Kilnamanagh	Cloonacarrow	9	RC	
		Kilnamanagh	9,15	EC	G

NGA No.	CIVIL PARISH	TOWNLAND OR TOWN, STREET	OS No.	CHURCH	GRAVE-YARD
40	Kilronan	Village of Ballyfarnan	1	M	
		Churchacres	4		G
		Derreenavoggy	2	RC	
		Glebe	4	EC	G
		Village of Keadew	4	RC	
41	Kilteevan	Cloontogher	40	RC	
		Kilteevan	40		G
42	Kiltoom	Cornaseer	48,49	RC	
				EC	
		Kiltoom	45,48		G
43	Kiltrustan	Kiltrustan	23		G
44	Kiltullagh	Ballinlough	25	EC	G
		Churchquarter	26		G
		Cloonfad West	31,32	RC	
		Garranlahanmore	32	RC	G
		Kiltullagh	25,32		G
		Stonepark South	32		G
45	Lissonuffy	Granaghan (Dillon)	29,30	RC	
		Lissonuffy	29		G
46	Moore	Cloonburren	54,56		G
		Cloonfad	56	RC	
		Kilbegley	54,56		G
		Loughlackagh	54	RC	
		Moore South	54		G
		Oldtown Kilcashel	54	EC	
47	Ogulla	Carrownageelaun	22,28	RC	
		Ogulla	22,28		G
		Tulsk	22,28		G
48	Oran	Carroweighter	34		G
49	Rahara	Rahara	43		G
				RC	
50	Roscommon	Roscommon, Church Lane	39	M	
				EC	
		Church Street		M	

COUNTY ROSCOMMON

NGA No.	CIVIL PARISH	TOWNLAND OR TOWN, STREET	OS No.	CHURCH	GRAVE-YARD
50	Roscommon	Roscommon, Church Street	39	Convent of Mercy Chapel	
		Main Street		RC	
		Main Street		RC	
51	St. Johns	Ballybrogan	45,46		G
		Killiaghan and Gort	45	RC	
		Rinnagan	42,43,46		G
52	St. Peters	Athlone, Chapel Lane	52	RC	
		College Lane		RC	
		King Street		EC	G
		Cloonakille	48,51 52		G
		Cloonown	52,55	RC	G
53	Shankill	Ballyroddy	16	RC	
		Edenan	16	RC	G
		Shankill	16		G
54	Taghboy	Ballyforan	47	RC unfinished	
		Carrownadurly	47	RC	
		Taghboy	44		G
55	Taghmaconnell	Bellaneeny	51	RC	
		Castlesampson	48,51		Infant G
		Killeglen	50		Infant G
		Taghmaconnell	51,54	EC	G
56	Termonbarry	Kilbarry	24,30		G
		Newtown	24,39	RC	
		Roosky	18,24	RC	
		Town of Roosky	18,24	EC	G
57	Tibohine	Cloonard	20		G
		Cloonshanville	15		G
		Creevy	13,14	RC	
		Curreentorpan	14,20		G

NGA No.	CIVIL PARISH	TOWNLAND OR TOWN, STREET	OS No.	CHURCH	GRAVE-YARD
57	Tibohine	Frenchpark, Roscommon Old Road	15	RC	
		Glebe West	20	EC	Old G
		Gortaganny	19	RC	
		Village of Loughglinn	20	RC	
		Mullaghnashee	14,20	RC	
		Portaghard	14,15	EC	
		Teevnacreeva	8,14	RC	
		Tibohine	14		G
58	Tisrara	Carrowntemple	44	RC	G
		Mount Talbot	44	EC	G
59	Tumna	Village of Battlebridge	7	EC	
		Cootehall	7	RC	
		Tumna	7,11		G

NGA No.	CIVIL PARISH	TOWNLAND OR TOWN, STREET	OS No.	CHURCH	GRAVE-YARD
1	Achonry	Achonry	32,38	EC	G
		Town of Bellahy	42	RC	
		Carrowntawa	32	RC	
		Cloonacool	24,31	RC	
		Curry	42,43	RC	
		Kilcummin	24,31		G
		Lavagh	32		G
		Montiagh	42		G
		Moylough	38,43	RC	
		Tobercurry	38	RC	G
		Town of Tobercurry		RC	
2	Aghanagh	Cuilsheeghary More	40	EC	
		Gortalough	40	RC	
3	Ahamlish	Ballinphull	2	RC	
		Grange	5	RC	
		Moneygold	5	EC	G
4	Ballynakill	Ballynakill	27		G
5	Ballysadare	Town of Ballysadare	20	EC	
		Halfquarter	20	RC	
		Kilboglashy	20		G
6	Ballysumaghan	Ballysumaghan	21,27	EC	
		Srananagh	27	EC	
7	Calry	Colgagh	15	RC	
		Sligo, Gore Street or The Mall	14	EC	
		Stephen Street		M	
				I	
8	Castleconor	Killanly	22	EC	
					G
		Rathglass	22	RC	
9	Cloonoghil	Ballynaraw South	38,39	RC	
		Rinnarogue	39		G
10	Dromard	Altanelvick	19	RC	
		Dromard	19		G

NGA No.	CIVIL PARISH	TOWNLAND OR TOWN, STREET	OS No.	CHURCH	GRAVE-YARD
10	Dromard	Tanrego East or Carrowmore	14	EC	G
11	Drumcliff	Ballinphull	4,5,8	EC	
		Carrigeens	4,7		G
		Cloughboley	7	RC	
		Drumcliff South	8	EC RC	G
		Drum West	8	M	
		Rosses Upper	8	EC	
12	Drumcolumb				
13	Drumrat	Kiltyteigh	39	RC	
		Knockbrack	39		G
14	Easky	Village of Easky	11	RC EC	G
15	Emlaghfad	Ballymote, Market Street	33	EC	G
		Market Street		RC	
		Mill Street		M	
		Emlaghfad	33,39		G
16	Kilcolman	Monasterredan	44,46		G
17	Kilfree	Carrowntemple	43,44 46		G
		Gorteen	44	EC	G
		Rathmadder	44	RC	
18	Kilglass	Carrowhubbock South	16		G
		Drinaghan More	17	RC	
		Kilglass	16	EC	G
19	Killadoon				
20	Killaraght	Cloonloogh	45	RC	
		Cuppanagh	45,47		G
		Rathtermon	47	RC	
21	Killaspugbrone	Drinaghan	14	RC	
		Killaspugbrone	13,14		G
		Larass or Strandhill	14	EC	G

NGA No.	CIVIL PARISH	TOWNLAND OR TOWN, STREET	OS No.	CHURCH	GRAVE- YARD
22	Killerry	Killerry	15,21		G
		Kingsfort	21	EC RC	
23	Killoran	Killoran North	25		G
		Rathbarran	25	EC	
		Shancough	25	RC	
24	Kilmacallan	Bellarush	34	RC	
		Cooperhill	27,34	EC	
		Village of Riverstown	27,34	RC	
25	Kilmacowen	Kilmacowen	22		G
26	Kilmacshalgan	Cloonascoffagh	12	EC	G
		Dunneill	12,18		G
		Farranmacfarrell	12,18	RC	
		Knockacullen	11,12	P	
27	Kilmacteige	Killure	36,37		G
		Kilmacteige	30,36	RC EC	
		Largan	30	RC	
		Toorlestraun	37	RC	
28	Kilmactranny	Ballynashee	35	RC	
		Carrickard	41	EC	G
		Highwood	35,41	RC	
29	Kilmoremoy	Ardnaree, Chapel Street	29	RC	
		Church Street		EC	G
30	Kilmorgan	Kilcreevin (Phibbs)	33	RC	
		Kilmorgan	34		G
31	Kilross	Ballydawley	20,21		G
		Kilross	21		G
32	Kilshalvy	Killavil	39	RC	
		Kilshalvy	39,44		G
33	Kilturra	Kilturra	38,39		G
34	Kilvarnet	Ballynacarrow North	26,33	RC	
35	Rossinver	Gortnahoula	3,6	RC in Progress	

NGA No.	CIVIL PARISH	TOWNLAND OR TOWN, STREET	OS No.	CHURCH	GRAVE-YARD
35	Rossinver	Lecklasser	3,6	RC	
36	St. Johns	Sligo, Abbey Street	14	Old Abbey	G
		Chapel Hill		Convent RC	
				RC	
		Church Lane		P	
		High Street		RC	
		John Street		St.Johns EC	G
37	Shancough				
38	Skreen	Leekfield	13,19	RC	
		Skreen More	13,19	EC	G
39	Tawnagh	Tawnagh	34		G
40	Templeboy	Ballyeeskeen	12,18	RC	
		Cashelboy	12,18		G
41	Toomour	Fallougher	39,40	RC	
		Graniamore	33,34	P	
		Templevanny	40		G

NGA No.	CIVIL PARISH	TOWNLAND OR TOWN, STREET	OS No.	CHURCH	GRAVE-YARD
1N	Abington				
1S	Aghacrew				
2N	Aghnameadle	Aghnameadle	22		G
		Blakefield	28	RC	
		Toomyvara, Church Street	22	EC	G
		Main Street			G
					G
				RC	
3N	Aglishcloghane	Feigh West	7	EC	G
		Lisheen	7	RC	
4N	Ardcrony	Ardcrony	15	RC	
					G
		Ballinderry	16	EC	
2S	Ardfinnan	Ardfinnan	82,88	EC	G
		Commons	88	RC	
3S	Ardmayle	Ardmayle	52	EC	G
		Nodstown	52,53	RC	
5N	Athnid				
6N	Ballingarry	Ballingarry	7,8,11	EC	G
		Ballynahinch	8,11	RC	
4S	Ballingarry	Ballingarry Lower	55	EC	G
		Village of Ballingarry, Commons Road	55	RC	G
5S	Ballintemple	Ballintemple	59,60	EC	G
				RC	
6S	Ballybacon	Carryduff	87,88	RC	
		Raheen	88		G
7N	Ballycahill	Ballycahill	40,41		G
		Castlefogarty	40	RC	
7S	Ballyclerahan	Ballyclerahan	76,77		G
		Village of Ballyclerahan	76,77	RC	
8N	Ballygibbon	Ballygibbon	15		G
8S	Ballygriffen	Ballygriffen	60		G
		Ballynahinch	52,60		G

COUNTY TIPPERARY

NGA No.	CIVIL PARISH	TOWNLAND OR TOWN, STREET	OS No.	CHURCH	GRAVE-YARD
9N	Ballymackey	Ballinree	21	RC	
		Cloonmore	21	EC	G
		Grenanstown	21,27	RC	
10N	Ballymurreen	Ballymurreen	47,48		G
11N	Ballynaclogh	Ballynaclogh	21,27	EC	G
		Ballyquiveen	27	RC	
9S	Ballysheehan	Carrow	53	EC	
		Rathclogh North	53,61	RC	
10S	Baptistgrange				
12N	Barnane-Ely				
11S	Barrettsgrange				
13N	Borrisnafarney	Borrisnafarney	22,28		G
14N	Borrisokane	Borrisokane, Church Street	10	EC	G
		Main Street		M	
		Mill Street		RC	
15N	Bourney	Ballyhenry	17	EC	G
		Ballykelly	18	Q	Quakers G
		Bawnmadrum North	17,18		G
		Clonakenny	23	RC	G
		Gorteen	23		G
		Shanballynahagh	17,23	RC	G
12S	Boytonrath	Boytonrath	68		G
13S	Brickendown	Brickendown	61		G
14S	Bruis	Bruis	66		G
15S	Buolick	Buolick	42,48		G
		Village of Gortnahoo	42,43	RC	
16N	Burgesbeg	Burgesbeg	19,25,26		G
16S	Caher	Ballybrada	81		Quakers G
		Caher, Abbey Street	75	Q	G
		Chapel Road		RC	
		Church Street		EC	
		Market Street			G

208

NGA No.	CIVIL PARISH	TOWNLAND OR TOWN, STREET	OS No.	CHURCH	GRAVE- YARD
16S	Caher	Loughlokery	76,82		G
17S	Carrick	Carrick-on-Suir, Chapel Lane	85	RC	
		Fair Green			Nunnery G
		Green Lane		RC	
		Main Street		EC	G
		Pill Road		RC Mount Saint Nicholas Monastery	G
17N	Castletownarra				
18S	Clogher	Clogher	46		G
18N	Cloghprior	Priorpark	9,14		G
19S	Clonbeg	Lisvarrinane	73	RC	
		Newtown	66,67, 73,74	EC	G
20S	Clonbulloge	Carriganagh	68		G
21S	Cloneen	Ballyhomuck	63,71	RC	G
22S	Clonoulty	Clonoulty Churchquarter	46,52	EC	G
		Clonoulty Curragh	46,52	RC	
		Drum	46	RC	G
23S	Clonpet				
24S	Colman	Colman (Hennessy)	69,70		G
25S	Cooleagh	Cooleagh	62		G
26S	Coolmundry				
19N	Corbally	Camlin	17	RC	G
		Cappalahan	18	EC	G
		Corville	12,17		G
		Cullaun	18		G
		Monaincha	12,17 18		G
		Rockforest	18	RC	
		Timoney	18		G
27S	Cordangan	Cordangan	67		G

NGA No.	CIVIL PARISH	TOWNLAND OR TOWN, STREET	OS No.	CHURCH	GRAVE-YARD
28S	Corroge				
29S	Crohane	Crohane Lower	54,55		G
30S	Cullen	Village of Cullen	58	RC	
		Oola Road		EC	G
20N	Cullenwaine				
31S	Dangandargan	Dangandargan	60,68		G
32S	Derrygrath	Woodroof	76	EC	
33S	Dogstown				
21N	Dolla	Curreeny Commons	32,33	RC	
34S	Donaghmore	Donaghmore	77		G
35S	Donohill	Churchfield	59		G
		Garryshane	59	RC	
		Rossacrow	51	RC	
22N	Doon				
23N	Dorrha	Derry	1,2, 4,5		G
		Graigue	5	EC	G
		Gurteen	2,5	RC	
36S	Drangan	Knockroe	63		G
		Newtowndrangan	63	RC	
24N	Drom	Drom	28,29, 34,35		G
				RC	
25N	Dromineer	Dromineer	14		G
37S	Emly	Village of Emly	65	EC	G
				RC	
38S	Erry				
39S	Fennor	Fennor	42,43	EC	G
26N	Fertiana				
40S	Fethard	Fethard, Abbey Street	70	St. Augustine Friary Chapel	
		Main Street		RC	
				EC	G

NGA No.	CIVIL PARISH	TOWNLAND OR TOWN, STREET	OS No.	CHURCH	GRAVE-YARD
40S	Fethard	Fethard, Moor Street	70	P	
27N	Finnoe	Ballyquinlevan Upper	9	RC	
		Curraghmore	10	EC	G
41S	Gaile				
28N	Galbooly	Galbooly	41,47, 48		G
42S	Garrangibbon				
43S	Glenbane				
29N	Glenkeen	Borrisoleigh, Chapel Street	34	RC	G
		Nenagh Road		EC	G
		Glenkeen	34		G
		Lismakeeve	34	RC	
44S	Grangemockler	Grangemockler	71,72	RC	
					G
45S	Graystown	Ballinure	53		G
30N	Holycross	Holycross	47	EC	G
				RC	G
46S	Horeabbey	Horeabbey	60,61		G
31N	Inch	Goldengrove	40		G
		Magherareagh	34		G
		Monroe	34,40	RC	
47S	Inishlounaght	Blackcastle	76		G
		Inishlounaght	83	EC	G
48S	Isertkieran	Ballynacloghy	63		G
32N	Kilbarron	Kilbarron	9		G
		Kilbiller	9	EC	
49S	Kilbragh				
50S	Kilcash	Kilcash	78		G
		Toor	78		G
33N	Kilclonagh				
34N	Kilcomenty	Birdhill	25,31	RC	
51S	Kilconnell				
35N	Kilcooly				
52S	Kilcooly	Bawnlea	49	BAP M	

NGA No.	CIVIL PARISH	TOWNLAND OR TOWN, STREET	OS No.	CHURCH	GRAVE-YARD
52S	Kilcooly	Glengoole South	48,54		G
		Graigaheesha	43		G
		Kilcoolyabbey	43	EC	
					G
		Village of New Birmingham, Main Street	48	RC	G
53S	Kilcornan				
54S	Kilfeakle	Kilfeakle Churchquarter	59		G
		Moatquarter	59,60, 67	RC	
		Thomastown Demesne North	59,60, 67,68		G
36N	Kilfithmone	Kilfithmone	34	EC	G
55S	Kilgrant	Mylerstown	78		G
		Powerstown	77,83	RC	
		Redmondstown	77,83	RC	
37N	Kilkeary	Kilkeary	21,27		G
56S	Killaloan	Killaloan Lower	83	EC	G
57S	Killardry	Glebe	75		G
		Kilmoyler	75	RC	
38N	Killavinoge	Clonmore	23,29	RC	
		Glebe	23,24		G
39N	Killea	Killea	29	RC	
		Park	23,29		G
58S	Killeenasteena				
59S	Killenaule	Killenaule, New Chapel Lane	54	RC	
		River Street		EC	G
		Lanespark	48,54		G
		Moglass	62	RC	
40N	Killodiernan	Johnstown	9,14	EC	
					G
		Village of Puckaun	14	RC	
41N	Killoscully	Garraunbeg	31,32	EC	G
		Killoscully	26,32	RC	G
42N	Killoskehan				

NGA No.	CIVIL PARISH	TOWNLAND OR TOWN, STREET	OS No.	CHURCH	GRAVE-YARD
43N	Kilmastulla	Kilmastulla	25	EC	
44N	Kilmore	Ballygown South	26	RC	
		Kilboy	26		G
		Kilmore	26		G
		Silvermines, Church Place	26	EC	G
60S	Kilmore				
61S	Kilmucklin				
62S	Kilmurry	Ballyneill	78,79, 84,85	RC	
					G
45N	Kilnaneave	Ballindigny	27	RC	
		Kilnaneave	27		G
46N	Kilnarath	Bleanbeg	32	RC	
		Newross	31		G
		Rossfinch	25,31	RC	
63S	Kilpatrick	Kilpatrick	51,59		G
47N	Kilruane	Kilruane	15	EC	G
		Lisgarode	15,21	RC	
64S	Kilshane	Kilshane	67		G
65S	Kilsheelan	Ballynaraha	78,84		G
		Gammonsfield	78,84	RC	
		Town of Kilsheelan	84		G
66S	Kiltegan	Kiltegan	77,83		G
67S	Kiltinan	Killusty North	70,71	RC	
		Kiltinan	70,77		G
48N	Kilvellane	Ballymackeogh	31,37		G
		Newport	31,37	EC RC	
68S	Kilvemnon	Kilvemnon	63,71		G
		Village of Mullinahone, Callan Street	63	RC	G
		Mullinoly	63	EC	
49N	Knigh	Knigh	14		G
69S	Knockgraffon	Graigue	68,69, 75,76	EC	

NGA No.	CIVIL PARISH	TOWNLAND OR TOWN, STREET	OS No.	CHURCH	GRAVE-YARD
69S	Knockgraffon	Loughkent Lower	69,76		G
		Loughkent West	68,69	RC	
50N	Latteragh	Latteragh	28		G
70S	Lattin	Ballynadruckilly	66	RC	
		Lattin West	66		G
71S	Lickfinn				
51N	Lisbunny	Lisbunny	20,21		G
72S	Lismalin	Lismalin	55,63		G
73S	Lisronagh	Lisronagh	77	RC	
				EC	G
52N	Lorrha	Village of Lorrha	4	EC	G
				RC	G
		Redwood	1,4	RC	
53N	Loughkeen	Caherhoereigh	5,8	RC	
		Loughkeen	8	EC	G
54N	Loughmoe East				
55N	Loughmoe West	Tinvoher	35	RC	
					G
74S	Magorban	Magorban	61	EC	G
75S	Magowry	Magowry	62,63		G
76S	Modeshill	Modeshill (Ayre)	55,56 63,64		G
56N	Modreeny	Cloghjordan, Church Street	15,16	EC	
		Main Street		M	
				M	
		Coolnamunna	15	RC	
		Modreeny	10,15	EC	G
77S	Molough	Moloughabbey	88		G
57N	Monsea	Monsea	14,20	RC	
				EC	G
78S	Mora				
79S	Mortlestown	Mortlestown	76		G
80S	Mowney				
58N	Moyaliff	Drumbane	40,46	RC	

NGA No.	CIVIL PARISH	TOWNLAND OR TOWN, STREET	OS No.	CHURCH	GRAVE-YARD
58N	Moyaliff	Glebe	40,46	EC	G
		Moyaliff	40,46		G
		Rosmult	40		G
59N	Moycarkey	Moycarkey	47	RC	Childrens G
					G
60N	Moyne	Cooleeny	36	EC	G
		Moynetemple	36	RC	G
81S	Neddans	Neddans (Farrans)	88		G
61N	Nenagh	Nenagh, Chapel Lane	20,21	RC	
		Church Street		EC	G
		Silver Street		M	
		Summerhill		CB	
		Tyone			G
82S	Newcastle	Clashganny West	88,94	RC	G
		Village of Newcastle	88,91		G
83S	Newchapel	Newchapel	76,77	EC	G
84S	Newtownlennon	Athenny	79		G
		Newtown Lower	79	RC	G
85S	Oughterleague	Clonaspoe	52	EC in Ruins	G
		Killenure	52,60	RC	
86S	Outeragh	Outeragh	75,76		G
87S	Peppardstown				
62N	Rahelty	Rahelty	35,36, 41,42		G
88S	Railstown	Railstown	61,69		G
89S	Rathcool	Ballintemple	62,70		G
90S	Rathkennan				
91S	Rathlynin				
63N	Rathnaveoge	Rathnaveoge Lower	17		G
92S	Rathronan	Rathronan	77	EC	G

NGA No.	CIVIL PARISH	TOWNLAND OR TOWN, STREET	OS No.	CHURCH	GRAVE-YARD
93S	Redcity	Redcity	70		G
94S	Relickmurry and Athassel	Athasselabbey North	60,68		G
		Ballyslatteen	68		G
		Village of Golden, Main Street	60	RC	
				EC	G
95S	Rochestown				
64N	Roscrea	Roscrea, Abbey Street	12	RC	G
		Church Street		EC	G
				M	
		The Mall		M	
		Rosemary Street		Q	
96S	St. Johnbaptist	Cashel, Friars Street	61	RC	G
		John Street		EC	G
					Part of G
		Main Street		M	
		Cooper's-Lot	61		G
97S	St. Johnstown	St. Johnstown	62		G
98S	St. Mary's Clonmel	Town of Clonmel	83		G
		Clonmel, Abbey Street		Chapel	
		Anglesea Street		P	
		Anne Street		EC	G
		Duncan Street		CB	
		Gordon Street		I	
				M	
		Irishtown		RC	
		Johnston Street		RC	
		Market Street		Q	
		Mary's Street		M	
		Morton Street		BAP	
		Nelson Street		P	
		New Street			Quakers G
		St. Stephen's Lane			St Stephen G

NGA No.	CIVIL PARISH	TOWNLAND OR TOWN, STREET	OS No.	CHURCH	GRAVE-YARD
99S	St. Patricksrock	Cashel, Chapel Lane	61		G
		The Rock		Ruins of EC	G
		Garryandrew South	69	RC	
100S	Shanrahan	Town of Burncourt	80,85	RC	
		Town of Clooneen, Main Street	87	EC	
				RC	
		Shanbally	86		G
		Shanrahan	87,90		G
101S	Shronell	Deerpark	66	EC	G
65N	Shyane	Clobanna	35,41		G
102S	Solloghodbeg				
103S	Solloghodmore	Ballyryan West	58	RC	G
66N	Templeachally	Ballina	25	RC	
		Roolagh	25		G
67N	Templebeg	Churchquarter	39	RC	G
104S	Templebredon	Knockalegan	57	RC	
68N	Templederry	Cloghonan	27,33	RC	
		Templederry	27	EC	G
69N	Templedowney				
105S	Temple-Etney	Ballypatrick	71,78	RC	
		Temple-Etney	77		G
106S	Templemichael	Templemichael	72		G
70N	Templemore	Kiltillane	29	EC	G
		Templemore Demesne	29		G
		Templemore, George's Street	29	M	
		Main Street		RC	
		Preaching Lane		M	
107S	Templeneiry	Village of Bansha	67	RC	
				EC	G
108S	Templenoe	Templenoe	59		G
71N	Templeree	Ballinroe	29,30		G
		Gorteendangan	29	RC	

NGA No.	CIVIL PARISH	TOWNLAND OR TOWN, STREET	OS No.	CHURCH	GRAVE-YARD
109S	Templetenny	Ballyporeen, Chapel Street	86	RC	
		Main Street		EC	
		Knocknagapple	86		G
72N	Templetouhy	Ballyknockane	29,30		G
		Longorchard	30,36	EC	G
		Village of Templetouhy, Chapel Street	30,36	RC	G
73N	Terryglass	Terryglass	6	RC	
				EC	G
		Village of Terryglass	6		G
74N	Thurles	Brittas	35,41		G
		Killinane	41		G
		Thurles, Church Lane	41	EC	G
		Garryvicleheen Street			St. Bridgets G
		Main Street		RC	G
				RC	
		Pudding Lane		RC	Christian Brothers G
		Turtulla Road		M	
110S	Tipperary	Tipperary, Church Lane	67	EC	G
		James Lane		P	
		Main Street		M	
		Nelson Street		RC	
		Murgasty	67		G
75N	Toem	Town of Cappaghwhite, Nenagh Road	51	RC	
		Clonmurragha	45	RC	
		Kilbeg	50,51	EC	G
111S	Tubbrid	Ballydrinan	81		G
		Knockane (Puttoge)	81	RC	
		Tubbrid	81,87	EC	G
112S	Tullaghmelan	Ballybeg	88	EC	
		Park	82	RC	

NGA No.	CIVIL PARISH	TOWNLAND OR TOWN, STREET	OS No.	CHURCH	GRAVE-YARD
112S	Tullaghmelan	Tullaghmelan	82,88		G
113S	Tullaghorton	Castlegrace	87	RC	G
114S	Tullamain	Rosegreen	69	RC	G
76N	Twomileborris	Ballybeg	48	EC	G
		Borris	42,48		G
		Village of Borris	42,48	RC	
77N	Upperchurch	Cappanaleigh	40	RC	G
78N	Uskane	Uskane	7		G
115S	Whitechurch	Whitechurch	81		G
79N	Youghalarra	Monroe	14,20	RC	
		Youghalvillage	14,20		G

COUNTY TYRONE

NGA No.	CIVIL PARISH	TOWNLAND OR TOWN, STREET	OS No.	CHURCH	GRAVE-YARD
1	Aghaloo	Caledon, Castle Lane	67	P	
		Church Hill	67	EC	
				M	
		Creevelough	61,67	EC	
		Crilly	66	P	G
				Meeting House	G
		Derrygooly	67	RC	G
		Lismulladown	66,67	P	G
2	Aghalurcher	Kiltermon	64	EC	
3	Arboe	Aghacolumb	39,40	EC	G
		Cluntoe (Richardson)	40	RC	
		Farsnagh	49		G
		Killycolpy	39,40	P	
		Mullanahoe	40	RC	G
4	Ardstraw	Carncorran Glebe	16,24	RC	
		Carnkenny	17	P	
		Cavandarragh	16,24	M	
		Clady Blair	10,17	P	
		Croshballinree	17	P	
		Drumclamph	16,24	EC	
		Drumlegagh	24,25	P	
		Envagh	24,25	RC	G
		Garvetagh Lower	24	P	
		Glenknock or Cloghogle	17	RC	
		Grange	17	P	
		Knockroe	10,17	P	
		Lisleen	24	M	
		Mulvin	10,17	P	
		Newtownstewart, Back Lane	17	M	
		Back Street		M	
		Main Street		EC	G
4	Ardstraw	Scarvagherin	16		G
		Tamnagh	25	EC	

NGA No.	CIVIL PARISH	TOWNLAND OR TOWN, STREET	OS No.	CHURCH	GRAVE-YARD
5	Artrea	Tullyraw	30,39	EC	G
6	Ballinderry	The Gort (Alias) Eglish	31		G
7	Ballyclog	Brigh	39	Meeting House	G
		Drumbanaway	39	RC	
		Glebe	39	EC	G
8	Bodoney Lower	Droit	18	P EC	G
		Gortin, Main Street	18	P	
		Greenan	19	EC	
		Rousky	19	RC	
		Sheskinshule	19,27	RC	
9	Bodoney Upper	Corickmore	18		G
		Eden Mill	11	P	
		Glenroan	11,12	EC	G
		Learden Lower	18	P	
		Lisnacreaght	11	RC	
		Oughtboy	7,12	RC	
10	Camus	Strabane, Barrack Street	4,5	M	
		Church Street		M	
		Irish Street		EC	G
		Meeting House Street		P	
		Townsend Street		RC	
11	Cappagh	Aghagallon	35,43	EC	
		Aghalane	26,27	EC	
		Dunmullan	26		G
		Killyclogher	35	RC	G
		Knockmoyle	25,26	RC	G
		Mountjoy Forest East Division	25,26, 35	EC	G
		Recarson	35	P	
		Tattraconnaghty	25	P	
					G
12	Carnteel	Aughnacloy, Caledon Street	60	M	
		Mill Street		M	
		Moore Street		EC	G

NGA No.	CIVIL PARISH	TOWNLAND OR TOWN, STREET	OS No.	CHURCH	GRAVE-YARD
12	Carnteel	Carnteel	60		G
		Dernabane	60	RC	
		Legaroe	53	P	
		Lisconduff	60	RC	
		Rousky	60		G
13	Clogher	Aghindrumman	58	RC	
		Ballaghneed	58	M	
		Ballynagurragh	59	RC	
		Carntall More	58	P	
		Clogher Demesne	58,59, 64,65	EC	G
		Clogher Tenements	58,59, 64		G
		Dunbiggan	51	EC	G
		Fivemiletown	63,64	M	
				EC	G
		Fivemiletown, Main Street	63,64	M	
		Lisnarab	51	RC	G
		Longridge	59	P	
		Syunshin	58,64	RC	
		Tatnadaveny	51,58	EC	
		Tullyquin Glebe	58	P	
14	Clogherny	Town of Beragh	43,44	RC	G
				M	
		Clogherny Glebe Lower	43,44		G
				EC	
		Dervaghroy	43	P	G
		Donaghane	35,43		G
		Seskinoe	43,51	RC	G
				P	G
15	Clonfeacle	Benburb	61	P	
				EC	G
		Derrygortrevy	61	EC	G
		Gorestown	61,62		G
		Grange	54,55,62	Q	

NGA No.	CIVIL PARISH	TOWNLAND OR TOWN, STREET	OS No.	CHURCH	GRAVE- YARD
15	Clonfeacle	Grange	54,55, 62		G
					Friends G
		Lisduff	61		G
		Moy, Chapel Lane	62	RC	G
				P	
		Charlemont Street		M	
		The Square		M	
				EC	G
				I	
		Mullycar	54,61	BAP	
		Roan	61	RC	G
		Stiloga	61		G
				P	
		Tullydowey	62	RC	G
16	Clonoe	Killary Glebe	47	EC	
		Magheralamfield	47	RC	
		Magheramulkenny	47	RC	
17	Derryloran	Cookstown, Church Street	29,38	EC	
		Coagh Road		3rd P	
		James Street		M	
				RC	
				1st P	
				2nd P	
				M	
		Glebe	38		G
		Gortalowry	29,38	RC	G
		Tullagh	29		G
18	Desertcreat	Desertcreat	38	EC	G
		Donaghrisk	38		G
		Edendoit	37	RC	
		Grange	38,39	COV	G
		Skenarget	38	Meeting House	
		Tullydonnell	38	RC	G

NGA No.	CIVIL PARISH	TOWNLAND OR TOWN, STREET	OS No.	CHURCH	GRAVE-YARD
19	Donacavey	Carryglass	57	EC	
		Cavan	42,50	M	
		Donacavey	51		G
		Ecclesville Demesne	50,51	RC	
				EC	
		Edenasop West	51	P	
		Fintona, Church Street	50,51	Ruins	G
		Main Street	51	M	
20	Donaghedy	Altrest	2	P	
		Bunowen	3		G
				EC	
		Cullion	2	COV	
		Dunnamanagh	3	P	
		Grange Foyle	2		G
		Killenny	6	RC	
		Sandville	2	P	
		Tamnabrady	1,2	P	
21	Donaghenry	Brackaville	46,47	M	
				EC	
				RC	
		Glebe	39		G
		Stewartstown, Back Row	39,47	P	
				RC	G
				M	
		Hill Head		P	
		North Street		EC	G
					G
22	Donaghmore	Village of Castlecaulfield	54	M	
				P	
		Town of Donaghmore	46	RC	
				EC	G
					Old G
		Drumreany	54	EC	G

NGA No.	CIVIL PARISH	TOWNLAND OR TOWN, STREET	OS No.	CHURCH	GRAVE-YARD
22	Donaghmore	Garvagh	46	P	
					G
		Gortnaglush	46	Meeting House	G
		Tullyallen	53	RC	G
23	Dromore	Aghadarragh	41,42, 49,50	RC	G
		Dromore	42,		G
		Drumskinny	49,50	M	
		Gardrum	42,50	P	
		Shanmullagh Glebe	50	EC	G
24	Drumglass	Dungannon, Ballygawley Road	54	P	
		Chapel Road		RC	
		Church Street		EC	G
		Perry Street		M	
		Scotch Street		P	
		Shamble Lane		M	
		Ross More	46		G
25	Drumragh	Ballynahatty	42,43	P	
		Drumragh(Caldwell)	43		G
		Fireagh(Gardiner)	34,42	RC	
		Gillygooly	34	P	
		Omagh, Ballygawley Road	35	P	
		Brook Street		RC	
		Church Street		M	
				EC	G
		Irish Town		M	
		New Street		P	
		Rakeeragh	42	P	
26	Errigal Keerogue	Ballygawley	52,53, 59,60	P	
		Ballynasaggart	52,59	EC	G
		Garvaghy	52	RC	G
		Gort	52,59		G
		Green Hill Demesne	52	RC	

NGA No.	CIVIL PARISH	TOWNLAND OR TOWN, STREET	OS No.	CHURCH	GRAVE-YARD
26	Errigal Keerogue	Knockonny	52	BAP	
		Lisnawery	59	M	
		Richmond	52,59	EC	G
27	Errigal Trough	Favor Royal Demesne	59	EC	
28	Kildress	Clare	29	EC	
		Dunnamore	28	RC	G
		Kildress Upper	29		G
		Killeenan	28	RC	G
		Tamlaght	29	P	G
29	Killeeshil	Ennish	53	P	
		Killeeshil	53	EC	G
		Kilskeery Glebe	56	EC	
		Lisfearty	53	P	
30	Killyman	Cavan	55	RC	
		Dungorman	55	M	
		Laghey	55	EC	
31	Kilskeery	Kilskeery Glebe	56	EC	
32	Learmount				
33	Leckpatrick	Artigarvan	5	P	
		Brownhill	5	RC	G
		Cloghcor	2	RC	G
		Leckpatrick	2,5	EC	G
		Strabane, Derry Road	5	P	
34	Lissan				
35	Longfield East	Drumquin, Meeting House Road	33,34	M P	
		Drumrawn	33,34	EC	G
36	Longfield West	Dooish	33,41	RC	G
		Lackagh	33		G
		Lisky Glebe	33	EC	G
37	Magheracross				
38	Pomeroy	Crossdernot	46	EC	G
		Galbally	45	RC	G

NGA No.	CIVIL PARISH	TOWNLAND OR TOWN, STREET	OS No.	CHURCH	GRAVE-YARD
38	Pomeroy	Pomeroy, The Diamond	37	EC	
				RC	G
		Main Street		P	G
39	Tamlaght	Coagh, Arboe Road	30,39	P	G
40	Termonamongan	Aghyaran	23	RC	G
		Magherakeel	23		G
		Magheranageeragh	23	P	G
		Speerholme	23	EC	G
41	Termonmaguirk	Aghogogan	36,37	RC	
		Creggan	27,28, 36	RC	
		Creggandevesky	36,37	RC	
		Drumduff	36,44	RC	
		Drumnakilly	35,36	EC	G
		Loughmacrory	27,36	RC	
		Six Mile Cross	44	P	G
				EC	G
		Village of Termon Rock	36	EC	G
42	Tullyniskan	Cullion	46	RC	
		Doras	46	EC	
		Drumreagh Otra	46	P	
43	Urney	Bridgetown	16,24	P	
		Castlederg, Main Street	16	M	
				EC	G
		Strabane Upper Road		P	
		Churchtown	16	RC	G
		Somervillestown	9	P	
		Strabane, Bridge End	5	RC	
		Urney Glebe	4,9	EC	G

NGA No.	CIVIL PARISH	TOWNLAND OR TOWN, STREET	OS No.	CHURCH	GRAVE-YARD
1	Affane	Affane Hunter	21,29	RC	
				EC	G
2	Aglish	Village of Aglish	29,34		G
				RC	G
		Village of Villierstown	29	EC	G
3	Ardmore	Village of Ardmore	38,40	RC	
		Ardocheasty	40		G
		Ballintlea North	39	RC	
		Ballintlea South	39		G
		Boherboy	38		G
		Dysert	40	EC	G
		Mountstuart	35	RC	
		Pulla	35,36		G
4	Ballygunner	Ballygunnercastle	18	RC	G
		Ballygunnertemple	18		G
5	Ballylaneen	Ballylaneen	24		G
		Carrigcastle	24	RC	G
6	Ballymacart	Ballymacart Upper	39	RC	
7	Ballynakill	Ballynakill	10,18	EC	G
8	Clashmore	Village of Clashmore	34,37	EC	G
		Coolbooa	37,38	RC	
9	Clongam	Curraghmore	3,4, 7,8	EC	G
10	Clonea				
11	Colligan	Colligan Beg	22		Old G
				RC	G
12	Corbally	Corbally Beg	27	RC	G
13	Crooke	Crooke	18		G
				RC	
14	Drumcannon	Drumcannon	17,26		G
		Tramore West	26	RC	G
		Tramore West, Church Road	26	EC	G
		Main Street		M	

NGA No.	CIVIL PARISH	TOWNLAND OR TOWN, STREET	OS No.	CHURCH	GRAVE-YARD
15	Dungarvan	Town of Abbeyside	31	RC	G
		Dungarvan, Buttery East	31	RC	G
				EC	G
		Church Street		Convent Chapel	
		St. Augustine Street		RC	
		Garrynageragh West	31	RC	G
		Kilminnin North	31		G
16	Dunhill	Village of Annestown	25	EC	G
		Dunhill	25	RC	G
					G
17	Dysert	Ballindysert	3	RC	
		Churchtown	2,3	EC	G
18	Faithlegg	Coolbunnia	10	RC	G
19	Fenoagh	Curraghnagarraha	3,4		G
20	Fews	Kilnagrange	15	RC	
21	Grange or Lisgennan	Mill and Churchquarter	38		G
		Tinnalyra	38	RC	
22	Guilcagh	Town of Portlaw	8	P	
				New Church	
23	Inishlounaught	Greenan	1	Convent RC Chapel	
24	Islandikane	Fennor North	25,26	RC	G
		Islandikane South	25,26		G
25	Kilbarry	Ballynaneashagh	9,17		G
		Kilbarry	9,17		G
26	Kilbarrymeadan	Village of Kill	25	RC	G
27	Kilbride				
28	Kilburne	Butlerstown South	17	RC	G
		Knockeen	17		G
29	Kilcaragh				
30	Kilcockan	Kilcockan	34		G
		Knockanore	34	RC	

NGA No.	CIVIL PARISH	TOWNLAND OR TOWN, STREET	OS No.	CHURCH	GRAVE-YARD
31	Kilcop				
	Kilculliheen	Abbeylands	9,10	RC	
				Old RC Chapel	G
		Abbeylands, Church Road	9,10	EC	G
32	Kilgobnet	Garranbaun	31	RC	G
		Kilbryan Lower	22,23	RC	
		Kilgobnet	31	RC	G
33	Killaloan				
34	Killea	Commons	27	RC	G
		Dunmore	27	EC	
35	Killoteran	Killoteran	9	EC	G
36	Kill St. Lawrence	Kill St. Lawrence	17		G
37	Kill St. Nicholas	Knockroe	18	EC	
38	Killure				
39	Kilmacleague				
40	Kilmacomb				
41	Kilmeadan	Ballyduff West	16	RC	
					G
		Coolfin	8	RC	G
					G
42	Kilmolash	Kilmolash	29,30		G
43		Carrickbeg	3		G
				RC	G
				Friary Chapel	G
44	Kilronan	Ballymacarbry	5	EC	
		Castlequarter	5	RC	
		Glebe	1		G
		Graignagowen	5		G
		Kilcreggane	5		G
45	Kilrossanty	Boolattin	23	RC	G
		Gortnalaght	14,15, 23,24	EC	G
		Kilrossanty	23		G

NGA No.	CIVIL PARISH	TOWNLAND OR TOWN, STREET	OS No.	CHURCH	GRAVE-YARD
46	Kilrush	Glebe	31		G
47	Kilsheelan				
48	Kilwatermoy	Churchquarter	28,33	RC	
		Fountain	29	EC	G
		Kilwatermoy	33		G
49	Kinsalebeg	Pilltown	37,38	RC	
		Prospecthall	37,40	EC	G
50	Leitrim				
51	Lickoran				
52	Lismore and Mocollop	Village of Ballyduff	20	RC	
		Cappoquin, Main Street	21	EC	G
		Mill Street		RC	
		Lismore	21	Convent Chapel	
		Lismore, Chapel Street	21	RC	G
		Main Street		P	
		North Mall		P	G
		Mocollop	19,20	EC	G
		Mountmelleray	12,21	RC	
		Townparks East	21,28, 29		G
53	Lisnakill	Lisnakill	17		G
54	Modelligo	Scart	22	RC	G
55	Monamintra				
56	Monksland	Ballynasissa	25	RC	G
		Ballyristeen	25	RC	G
57	Mothel	Ballyneal	7	RC	G
		Mothel	3,7	EC	G
58	Newcastle	Ardeenloun East	16		G
59	Rathgormuck	Carrowleigh	3,7	RC	G
		Rathgormuck	3		G
60	Rathmoylan				
61	Reisk	Reisk	17,26		G
62	Ringagonagh	Shanacloon	36	EC	G
		Shanakill	36	RC	G

NGA No.	CIVIL PARISH	TOWNLAND OR TOWN, STREET	OS No.	CHURCH	GRAVE-YARD
63	Rossduff				
64	Rossmire	Kilmacthomas	15	EC	G
		Parkeennalogh	15	RC	G
65	St. Marys Clonmel	Glebe	1		G
66	Seskinan	Knockaunbrandaun	5,6	RC	
		Knockboy	13		G
		Tooraneena	13		G
67	Stradbally	Carrickahilla	24	RC	
		Faha	15,24	RC	
68	Tallow	Tallow, Chapel Street or Bog Lane	28	RC	G
		Cockpit Lane		M	
		Tallowbridge Street		RC	
		West Street		EC	G
69	Templemichael	Ballyrussel	37	RC	
		Templemichael	37	EC	G
70	Waterford City				
70a	St. Johns Within	Waterford, Beresford Street	9	St.Johns RC Chapel (new)	
		Johns Lane			G
					G
		Manor Street		St.Johns RC Chapel (old)	
		Parliament Street			Friends G
70b	St. Johns Without	Ballymacarbry	9,17	RC	
		Waterford, Johns Lane	9		Friends G
		Lower Newton Road			Friends G
70c	St. Michaels	Town of Waterford, Michael Street	9		G
70d	St. Olaves	Waterford, Apartments Place	9	Friary RC	

NGA No.	CIVIL PARISH	TOWNLAND OR TOWN, STREET	OS No.	CHURCH	GRAVE-YARD
70d	St. Olaves	Waterford, Lady Lane	9	P	
		Peter Street		St.Olaves EC	
70e	St. Patricks	Waterford, Barron Strand Street	9	Part of RC Cathedral	
		Chapel Street		RC	
		Patrick Street		St.Patrick EC	G
70f	St. Peters	Waterford, Lady Lane	9	M	
				Convent	
				D	
70g	St. Stephens Within	Waterford, New Street	9		G
		Stephens Street		BAP	
70h	St. Stephens Without				
70i	Trinity Within	Waterford, Cathedral Square	9	P	
		Chapel Lane		RC Part of	
		French Church Street		Holy Ghost Institu- tion	
		The Quay		M	
70j	Trinity Without	Borheenclogh	9	Convent RC Chapel	
		Waterford, Barrack Street	9	Friary Chapel	G
		Beresford Street		P	
		Catherine Street		I	
		Chapel Lane		Bally- bricken RC	G
		King Street		Q	
		Thomas Hill			G
71	Whitechurch	Ballykennedy	30	EC	G
		Ballynameelagh	30	RC	

NGA No.	CIVIL PARISH	TOWNLAND OR TOWN, STREET	OS No.	CHURCH	GRAVE-YARD
1	Ardnurcher or Horseleap	Ardnurcher	31	EC	
		Kilbeg	31,37	RC	
2	Ballyloughloe	Labaun	30	EC	G
		Tullaghanshanlin	30	RC	
3	Ballymore	Ballymore	23,24	EC	G
		Ballymore, Main or High Street	24	RC	
4	Ballymorin	Ballymorin	17	EC	G
5	Bunown	Bunown	22		G
		Portlick	22		G
				EC	G
6	Carrick	Carrick	26,33		G
7	Castlelost	Castlelost	33		G
		Gallstown	33		G
		Town of Rochfortbridge	33	EC	
13	Castletowndelvin	Archerstown	8,9		G
		Village of Castletowndelvin	14	EC	G
				RC	
		Crowinstown Great	9,14		G
		Killadoughran	8,13		G
8	Castletownkindalen	Balrath	32		G
		Castletown	25,32	RC	
		Village of Castletown	32	EC	G
9	Churchtown	Churchtown	25	EC	G
10	Clonarney	Clonarney	9		G
11	Clonfad	Clonfad	32,33		G
		Meedian	33	RC	
		Village of Tyrellspass, Crescent	39	EC	G
		Main Street		M	
12	Conry	Togherstown	24,25	RC	
13	Delvin	See Castletowndelvin			
14	Drumraney	Cartroncoragh	23	EC	G
		Drumraney	23	RC	
15	Durrow				

NGA No.	CIVIL PARISH	TOWNLAND OR TOWN, STREET	OS No.	CHURCH	GRAVE-YARD
16	Dysart	Ballyote	18	RC	
		Dysart	25		G
		Rathnamuddagh	25	RC	
17	Enniscoffey	Enniscoffey or Caran	26,27	EC	G
18	Faughalstown	Faughalstown	7		G
		Milltown	7	RC	
19	Foyran	Foyran	1		G
		Togher	1	EC	
20	Kilbeggan	Kilbeggan	38	EC in ruins	G
		Kilbeggan, Chapel Road Church Lane	38	RC M EC	G
21	Kilbixy	Town of Ballynacarrigy, Main Street	10,11	RC	
		Baronstown Demesne	6,11	EC	G
		Tristernagh	11		Temple-cross G
22	Kilbride	Whitewell	26,33	EC in ruins	G
23	Kilcleagh	Ballynahoun	35	RC	
		Boggagh (Fury)	36	RC	
		Town of Moate, Main Street	30	Q EC RC	G G
24	Kilcumny	Kilcumny	8,13		G
		Loughstown	8	EC	
25	Kilcumeragh	Ballybrickoge	31	RC	
		Kilcumreragh	31	EC in ruins	G
26	Kilkenny West	Ballynacliffy	15		G
		Glassan	22	EC	
		Kilkenny Abbey	23	EC	G
		Toberclare	22	RC	
27	Killagh	Killagh	13,20, 21		G
28	Killare	Bracknahevla	24,31	RC	
		Killarechurch	24		G

NGA No.	CIVIL PARISH	TOWNLAND OR TOWN, STREET	OS No.	CHURCH	GRAVE-YARD
29	Killua	Village of Clonmellon, Main Street	9	RC	
				EC	G
30	Killucan	Corbetstown	20		G
		Crossanstown	27	RC	
		Glebe	20	EC	G
		Grange Beg	21,28		G
		Griffinstown	27		G
		Town of Kinnegad	27,28	RC	
				EC	G
		Village of Raharney	20,21	RC	
		Rathwire Lower	20,27	RC	
		Rathwire Upper	20,27	P	
31	Killulagh	Killulagh	13		G
		Mulchanstown	13	RC	
32	Kilmacnevan	Churchtown	10	RC	
					G
33	Kilmanaghan	Moate, Dublin Road	30	M	
		Newtown	30	M	
				RC	
34	Kilpatrick	Kilpatrick	8,13		G
35	Lackan	Lackan	6		G
				RC	
		Leny	6,11	EC	G
36	Leny				
37	Lickbla	Castletown Lower	1	RC	G
		Lickbla	3		G
38	Lynn	Catherinestown	26		G
		Gainestown	26	RC	
		Lynn	19,26	Old EC	G
39	Mayne	Fearmore	3	RC	
		Mayne	2,3	EC	G
40	Moylisker	Anneville or Rathduff	26	EC	G

NGA No.	CIVIL PARISH	TOWNLAND OR TOWN, STREET	OS No.	CHURCH	GRAVE-YARD
41	Mullingar	Brottonstown	18	RC	
		Church Island	12		G
		Culleen More	9,12		G
		Hopestown	18		G
		Marlinstown	19,26		G
		Mullingar, Back of the town	19	RC	
		Church Street		EC	G
		Harbour Street		P	G
		Meeting House Lane		M	
		Robinstown (Levinge)	19		G Attached to Workhouse
		Tuitestown	18,25		G
		Walshestown North	18	RC	
42	Multyfarnham	Abbeyland	6,7	RC	G
		Village of Multyfarnham	6,7	RC	G
43	Newtown	Ardmorney	38	RC	
		Cornaher	38,39	EC	
		Knockycosker	32	M	
		Newtownlow	38	EC in ruins	G
44	Noughaval	Clogher	16	RC	
		Clonkeen	15,16		G
		Island of Inchbofin	15		G
		Noughaval	16		G
45	Pass of Kilbride	Milltown	33,34	RC	
		Pass of Kilbride	27,34		G
46	Piercetown	Ballincurra	17	RC	
		Relick (Longworth)	10,17		G
47	Portloman	Portloman	11,18		G
48	Portnashangan	Ballynagall	12	EC	G
		Portnashangan	12		G
49	Rahugh	Kiltober	38	BAP	
		Montrath	38,39	RC	

NGA No.	CIVIL PARISH	TOWNLAND OR TOWN, STREET	OS No.	CHURCH	GRAVE-YARD
49	Rahugh	Rahugh	38,40	EC in ruins	G
50	Rathaspick	Joanstown	6,11	RC	
		Rataspick	5,6		G
		Rathowen	6	EC	G
51	Rathconnell	Balreagh	12,13		G
		Clonlost	20		G
		Crosserdree	13		G
		Rathconnell	19		G
		Reynella	13,20	EC	G
		Tevrin	13,20	RC	
52	Rathconrath	Corkan	17	RC	
		Killahugh	18	EC	G
53	Rathgarve	Castlepollard, Fore Street or Chapel Road	3,7	RC	
		Market Square		EC	
		Rathgarve	3		G
54	Russagh	Russagh	6		G
55	St. Feighins	Village of Collinstown	8	RC	
				EC	
		Fore	4,8		G
				RC	G
56	St. Mary's				
57	St. Mary's (Athlone)	Athlone	29	Abbey Ruins	G
		Athlone, Ballymahon Road	29	RC	
		Church Street		EC	G
		Court Devenish Lane (Off North Gate Street)		M	
		Friary Lane (Off Church Street)		Friary RC	
		Lloyd's Street (Off Church Street)		P	
		North Gate Street		M	
		Scotch Parade		BAP	
58	Stonehall	Stonehall	7,12	EC	G

NGA No.	CIVIL PARISH	TOWNLAND OR TOWN, STREET	OS No.	CHURCH	GRAVE-YARD
59	Street	Barradrum	2,6	EC	G
		Boherquill	2	RC	
60	Taghmon	Glebe	12	EC	G
		Toberaquill	12		G
61	Templeoran	Piercefield or Templeoran	11		G
		Sonna Demesne	11,18	RC	
62	Templepatrick	Village of Moyvore	17	P	
63	Tyfarnham	Kilmaglish	12		G
		Parsonstown	12	RC	

NGA No.	CIVIL PARISH	TOWNLAND OR TOWN, STREET	OS No.	CHURCH	GRAVE-YARD
1	Adamstown	Adamstown	31	RC	G
		Templeshelin	30	EC	G
2	Ambrosetown	Ambrosetown	46		G
3	Ardmine	Ballyduff Lower	17	EC	
		Village of Riverchapel	12	RC	
4	Ardcanrisk	Ardcanrisk	37		G
5	Ardcavan	Ardcavan	37,38		G
		Castlebridge	32,33	RC	
6	Ardcolm	Ardcolm	38		G
		Village of Castlebridge	37	EC	G
7	Artramon	Artramon	37		G
8	Ballingly	Ballingly	40,41		G
9	Ballyanne	Ballyanne	29		G
		Gobbinstown	30	RC	G
10	Ballybrazil	Ballybrazil	34,39		G
		Ballykeerogemore	39		G
11	Ballybrennan	Ballybrennan Big	48		G
12	Ballycanew	Ballycanew	16,17	RC	
		Town of Ballycanew	16,17	EC	
				M	
				EC	G
13	Ballycarney	Ballycarney	15	EC	G
		Mountfin Upper	14	RC	G
		Scarawalsh	20		G
		Tomgarrow	14,15		G
14	Ballyconnick	Ballyconnick	41		G
15	Ballyhoge	Gallbally	31	RC	G
16	Ballyhuskard	Ballymurry	27	RC	G
		Ballynastraw	26	RC	G
		Cooladine	26	Q	
		Kilcottybeg	26	EC	
17	Ballylannan	Ballylannan	40,45		G
		Rosegarland	40,45	Meeting House	

NGA No.	CIVIL PARISH	TOWNLAND OR TOWN, STREET	OS No.	CHURCH	GRAVE- YARD
18	Ballymitty	Hilltown	40	RC	
19	Ballymore	Grahormick	47		G
20	Ballynaslaney				
21	Ballyvaldon				
22	Ballyvaloo				
23	Bannow	Bannow	45		G
		Danescastle	45,46	RC	
24	Carn	Churchtown	53	EC	G
25	Carnagh	Carnagh	35		G
		Cushenstown	25	RC	G
26	Carnew	Askamore	5	RC	G
27	Carrick	Ballygoman	37	RC	G
		Newtown	37		G
28	Castle – Ellis	Castle – Ellis	27	EC	
29	Chapel	Ballymackesy	25	RC	
30	Clone	Ballysimon	20	RC	G
		Clone	15		G
		Solsborough	20	EC	G
					Quaker G
31	Clongeen	Clongeen	40	RC	
					G
32	Clonleigh	Donard	24	RC	G
33	Clonmines	Clonmines	45		G
34	Clonmore	Ballybuckley	25	EC	
		Bree	25		G
		Clonmore	31	RC	
					G
35	Coolstuff	Coolstuff	36		G
36	Crosspatrick				
37	Donaghmore	Ballygarrett	17	RC	
		Clonevin	17	EC	
		Donaghmore	17	EC	
38	Doonooney				

NGA No.	CIVIL PARISH	TOWNLAND OR TOWN, STREET	OS No.	CHURCH	GRAVE-YARD
39	Drinagh	Drinagh South	42		G
40	Duncormick	Duncormick	46	EC	G
		Rathangan	46	RC	
41	Edermine	Glebe	26	EC	G
		Mullinnagore Oilgate	32	RC	
42	Ferns	Town of Ferns, Chapel Street	15	RC	
		Main Street		EC	G
43	Fethard	Dungulph	45	RC	
		Grange	45,50	EC	G
		Town of Fethard	45,50	M	
44	Hook	Churchtown	54		G
45	Horetown	Cullenstown	35,36	RC	
		Horetown South	36,41	EC	G
46	Inch	Inch	3	EC	G
		Kayle	40		G
47	Ishartmon	Ballyboher	47		G
48	Kerloge				
49	Kilbride	Ballintore	15	Q	
50	Kilbridgelynn	Kilcaysan	16	RC	
51	Kilcavan	Balloughton	46	RC	
				EC	G
		Borleigh	3		G
		Kilcavan	46		G
52	Kilcomb	Ballyduff	10	RC	G
53	Kilcormick	Ballincash Upper	21	EC	G
		Kilcormick	21		G
		Tobergal	16	Old RC	G
				RC	
54	Kilcowan	Hooks	46		G
55	Kilcowanmore	Ballybrennan	31		G
56	Kildavin	Kildavin Lower	42		G
		Murntown Lower	42	RC	
57	Kilgarvan	Carrowreagh	36	RC	
		Kilgarvan	36		G

NGA No.	CIVIL PARISH	TOWNLAND OR TOWN, STREET	OS No.	CHURCH	GRAVE-YARD
58	Kilgorman	Ballynacree	7	RC	G
		Kilgorman	7		G
59	Killag	Killag	46,51,52		G
60	Killann	Grange Upper	18	RC	
		Killann	18,19	EC	G
61	Killegney	Castleboro Demesne	24,25	EC	
62	Killenagh				
63	Killesk	Drillistown	39		G
64	Killiane	Ballykelly	42	RC	
		Killiane Little	43		G
65	Killila	Ballynaglogh	27	RC	G
66	Killincooly				
67	Killinick	Ballyminaun Little	47	RC	
		Sanctuary	47	EC	G
68	Killisk	Killisk	27		G
69	Killurin	Bolabaun	37	RC	G
		Killurin	31,32,37	EC	G
70	Kilmacree	Kilmacree	42		G
71	Kilmakilloge	Clonatin Upper	7		G
		Town of Gorey,Ballycanew New Road	7	Convent RC	
		Bridge Row			G
		Church Lane			G
		Main Street		M EC	
		William Street		CAL	
72	Kilmallock	Ballymurn Upper	26,32	RC	
		Kilmallock	32		G
73	Kilmannan	Cleristown North	42	RC	
		Glebe	42		G
74	Kilmokea	Greatisland	39		G
		Horeswood	39	RC	

NGA No.	CIVIL PARISH	TOWNLAND OR TOWN, STREET	OS No.	CHURCH	GRAVE-YARD
75	Kilmore	Sarshill	52	RC	
76	Kilmuckridge	Kilmuckridge	22	EC	G
		Littermore	22	RC	
77	Kilnahue	Kilnahue	6		G
		Mangan	6	EC	G
		Monaseed Demesne	6	RC	G
78	Kilnamanagh	Ballinvack	21	EC	G
79	Kilnenor	Glebe	2,3		G
		Oulart	2	RC	G
80	Kilpatrick	Kyle Upper	32	EC	
		Sion	32	RC	G
81	Kilpipe	Barnadown	1,2		G
82	Kilrane	Churchtown	48	RC	
					G
83	Kilrush	Ballinapark	9	RC	
		Ballynaberny	10	EC	G
		Knockaree	10	RC	G
84	Kilscanlan				
85	Kilscoran	Kilscoran	48	EC	G
86	Kiltennell	Courtown	12	EC	
		Prospect	7		G
87	Kiltrisk				
88	Kilturk	Glebe	52	EC	
89	Ladyisland	Eardownes Great	48	RC	
90	Liskinfere	Ballinclay	11		Quakers G
		Churchtown	11	EC	
		Toberanieran	11		G
91	Maudlintown	Maudlintown	37		G
92	Mayglass	Courtlands West	47	RC	
		Glebe	47		G
93	Meelnagh	Kyle	21	RC	
94	Monamolin	Barraglan	16	RC	G
		Glebe	16,21	EC	G

NGA No.	CIVIL PARISH	TOWNLAND OR TOWN, STREET	OS No.	CHURCH	GRAVE-YARD
95	Monart	Caim	19	RC	
		Marshalstown	19,20	RC	G
		Newtown	19	RC	
		Pullinstown Big	19	EC	G
96	Moyacomb				
97	Mulrankin	Churchtown	47	EC	
		Common	47	RC	
98	Newbawn	Courthoyle New	30	RC	G
		Courthoyle Old	35		G
		Newbawn	35	RC	G
99	Oldross	Millquarter	30	EC	G
100	Owenduff	Nash	35		G
		Rathumney	39,40	RC	G
		Yoletown	40		G
101	Rathaspick	Rathaspick	42	EC	G
102	Rathmacknee	Pollsallagh	42	RC	
		Rathmacknee	42	EC	G
103	Rathroe				
104	Rossdroit	Cortnacuddy	25	RC	
		Davidstown	25	RC	G
		Moneytucker	25	EC	G
105	Rosslare	Churchtown	48		G
		Grahormack	48	RC	
106	Rossminoge	Island Upper	6	RC	
		Rossminoge North	11		G
107	St. Helen's				
108	St. Iberius	Allenstown Little	48	M	
		St. Iberius	48		G
109	St. James and Dunbrody	Ballyhack	44	EC	G
		Dunbrody	39		G
		Town of Duncannon	44		G
		Ramsgrange	44	RC	

NGA No.	CIVIL PARISH	TOWNLAND OR TOWN, STREET	OS No.	CHURCH	GRAVE-YARD
110	St. John's	St. John's	26		G
		Townparks	37	RC Convent RC	
		Wexford, Bowe Street Upper	37	RC in Progress	
		John Street			G
111	St. Margaret's	Begerin Island	38		G
		Kilmacoe	33	RC	
		St. Margaret's	53		G
112	St. Mary's (Enniscorthy)	Enniscorthy	20		G
		Enniscorthy, Church Street	20	EC	
		Duffrey Street		RC	
		Friary Lane		M	
		Rose Hill		Convent RC	
113	St. Mary's (New Ross)	Bishopsland	29	RC	
		Butlersland	29		G
		Morrissysland	29		G
		New Ross, Church Lane	29	EC	G
		High Hill(off North Street)		RC	G
		Marsh Lane		M	
		Priory Lane		Q	
		Robert Street		M	
		South Street		RC EC	
114	St. Mary's (Newtownbarry)	Ballyphilip	9,14	RC	G
		Newtownbarry, Church Street	9	EC	G
		Market Square		M	
115	St. Michael's	Bush	48		G
116	St. Mullin's				
117	St. Nicholas	Bishopland	33		G
118	St. Peter's				
119	Skreen	Ballymore	33	RC	G

NGA No.	CIVIL PARISH	TOWNLAND OR TOWN, STREET	OS No.	CHURCH	GRAVE- YARD
120	Tacumshin	Churchtown	53	EC	G
		Fence	53	RC	
121	Taghmon	Ballyshelin	41	RC	
		Coolow	41		G
		Forest	36	Q	G
		Taghmon	41		G
		Taghmon, Chapel Street	36	RC	
		Church Street		EC	G
		High Street	41		G
		Tincurra	41		G
122	Tellarought	Tellarought	34	RC	
123	Templeludigan	Templeludigan	24	RC	
				EC	G
124	Templescoby	Templescoby	19	EC	
125	Templeshanbo	Ballindaggan	14		G
		Bolabeg	14	EC	G
		Coolycarney	14,19	RC	G
		Village of Kiltealy	13	RC	
126	Templeshannon	Enniscorthy, Killagoley Lane	26	Q	
		The Shannon			G
127	Templetown	Kilcloggan	49	RC	
		Templetown	49	EC	G
				RC	
128	Tikillin	Tikillin	37		G
129	Tintern	Ballycullane	40	RC	G
		Kinnagh	45		G
		Saint Leonards	45	RC	
		Tintern	45		G
				EC	
130	Tomhaggard	Tomhaggard	47	RC	
					G
131	Toome	Ballinclare	11		G
		Balloughter	11	RC	G

NGA No.	CIVIL PARISH	TOWNLAND OR TOWN, STREET	OS No.	CHURCH	GRAVE-YARD
131	Toome	Town of Camolin	11	RC	G
				EC	G
				M	
132	WEXFORD CITY				
a	St. Bridget's	Bride Street	37	RC in Progress	
b	St. Doologe's				
c	St. Iberius	Anne Street		P	
		Main Street South		EC	
		Rowe Street		M	
d	St. Mary's	Mary's Lane		RC	G
e	St. Michael's of Feagh	Castle Hill			G
f	St. Patrick's	High Street		Q	
		Patrick Street			G
g	St. Peter's	School Street		RC	G
		Francis Street		Convent RC	
h	St. Selskar's	Temperance Row		EC	G
133	Whitechurch	Ballykelly	34	RC	
		Whitechurch	34,39	EC	G
134	Whitechurchglynn	Corlican	31,32		G
		Wilkinstown	36		G

NGA No.	CIVIL PARISH	TOWNLAND OR TOWN, STREET	OS No.	CHURCH	GRAVE-YARD
1	Aghowle	Aghowle Lower	42		G
		Coolkenna	42	EC	G
2	Ardoyne	Ardoyne	42		G
				EC	G
3	Arklow	Arklow, Abbey Lane	40,45		G
				M	
		Main Street			G
				RC	
				EC	
		Ballinabanoge	45		G
		Kilcarra West	40		G
4	Ballinacor	Ballinacor	29	RC	G
		Ballinatone Lower	29,30	EC	G
		Rosahane	29,34		G
5	Ballintemple	Ballintemple	40		G
				EC	
		Ballykillageer Upper	39,40	RC	G
6	Ballykine	Bahana (Whaley)	34,35		G
		Macreddin West	34	RC	G
					G
7	Ballynure	Ballynure	14,20	EC	G
		Village of the Grange	20	RC	
		Knockarrig	20		G
8	Baltinglass	Baltinglass East	27	RC in progress	
		Baltinglass, Chapel Hill	27	RC	G
		Baltinglass West	26,27	M	
		Coolinarrig Upper	27		G
		Deerpark	27		G
9	Blessington	Blessington, Main Street	5	EC	G
		Crosscoolharbour	5		G
10	Boystown	Boystown or Baltyboys Upper	10		G
					Quaker G
		Lackan	5,10		G

COUNTY WICKLOW

NGA No.	CIVIL PARISH	TOWNLAND OR TOWN, STREET	OS No.	CHURCH	GRAVE-YARD
10	Boystown	Lackan	5,10	RC	
		Valleymount or Cross	10	RC	
11	Bray	Bray, Church Terrace	4	EC	G
		Main Street		RC	
				P	
				M	
12	Burgage	Burgage More	5		G
13	Calary	Calary Upper	7,12	EC	G
14	Carnew	Ballard	43	EC	G
		Carnew, Carnew Street	47	M	
				EC	G
				I	
		Cronyhorn Upper	47		G
		Deerpark	43,47	RC	
					G
15	Castlemacadam	Castlemacadam	35	EC	G
		Kilmag	35,40		G
		Village of Newbridge	35	RC	G
		Templelusk	35,40		G
16	Crecrin	Ballyconnell	37	RC	
17	Crehelp				
18	Crosspatrick	Coolafancy	43,44	M	
				RC	G
				EC	G
19	Delgany	Delgany	8,13	RC	
		Town of Delgany	13	EC	G
					G
20	Derrylossary	Ballinacor	18	EC	G
		Brockagh	17,23,32	RC	
		Drummin	11,17,18	RC	
		Laragh East	17,18,23,24	EC	
		Village of Laragh	17,32	RC	

NGA No.	CIVIL PARISH	TOWNLAND OR TOWN, STREET	OS No.	CHURCH	GRAVE-YARD
20	Derrylossary	Sevenchurches or Camaderry	16,17, 22,23		G
		Togher More	18	RC	
21	Donaghmore	Donaghmore	21	EC	
		Kelshamore	21	RC	
		Leitrim	22		G
22	Donard	Donard Lower	21		G
		Town of Donard	15,21	EC	G
				RC	
23	Drumkay	Wicklow, Chapel Street	25	RC	
24	Dunganstown	Ballinacor West	31	RC	
		Ballymurrin Lower	31		Quaker G
				RC	
		Castletimon	31,36		G
		Dunganstown West	31	EC	
		Threemilewater	31		G
25	Dunlavin	Town of Dunlavin	15	EC	G
				RC	
					G
		Tornant Lower	15		G
26	Ennereilly	Ennereilly	41		G
27	Freynestown				
28	Glenealy	Ballymoat	24		G
				RC	
				EC	G
29	Hacketstown	Knockananna	33	RC	
30	Hollywood	Ballysize Lower	9		G
		Dragoonhill	9,15	EC	G
		Dunboyke	15		G
		Hollywood Upper	9	RC	G
31	Inch	Johnstown Upper	45	RC	
32	Kilbride	Athdown	6		G
		Ballinaheese	40	EC	
		Barranisky West	35,40	RC	G

NGA No.	CIVIL PARISH	TOWNLAND OR TOWN, STREET	OS No.	CHURCH	GRAVE-YARD
32	Kilbride	Cloghleagh	2,5,6	EC	
		Kilbride	1,5,	RC	
					G
					G
		Templemichael	40		G
		Templerain	40		G
				RC	
33	Kilcommon	Bahana	30		G
		Bridgeland	38	RC	
		Tinahely, Main Street	38	M	
		Whitefield	38	RC	
					G
34	Kilcoole	Kilcoole	13		G
		Kilquade	13	RC	
35	Killahurler	Mooreshill	39,40		G
36	Killiskey	Ballinahinch	25	RC	
		Ballyhenry	19		G
		Ballymaghroe	18,19, 24,25		G
		Clora	18,19, 24,25	EC	G
		Killiskey	19		G
37	Kilmacanoge	Village of Kilmacanoge	7	RC	
					G
38	Kilpipe	Curraghlawn	39	EC	
39	Kilpoole	Wickow, Bayview Terrace	25	Meeting House un-finished	
		Main Street		M	
40	Kilranelagh	Colvinstown Upper	27		G
		Talbotstown Upper	27	RC	
41	Kiltegan	Killamoat Lower	23	RC	
		Kiltegan	22		G
				EC	G
		Slievereagh Lower	28		G
42	Knockrath	Claramore	24	RC	

NGA No.	CIVIL PARISH	TOWNLAND OR TOWN, STREET	OS No.	CHURCH	GRAVE-YARD
42	Knockrath	Knockrath Little	23,24 29,30	EC	
43	Liscolman	Liscolman	37		G
44	Moyacomb	Balisland	46,47		G
45	Moyne	Askanagap	33,34	RC	
		Moyne	33	EC	
46	Mullinacuff	Kilquiggin	37,38, 42,43	RC	
		Knockatomcoyle	38,43	EC	
		Stranakelly	38,43		G
47	Newcastle Lower	Killadreenan	19		G
		Newcastle Middle	13,19	EC	
48	Newcastle Upper	Kilmurry	12,13, 18	RC	
		Town of Newtown Mountkennedy	13	EC	G
49	Powerscourt	Curtlestown Lower	7	RC	
		Powerscourt Demesne	7	EC	G G
50	Preban	Kilballyowen	39	M RC	
		Preban	39		G
51	Rathbran	Goldenfort	20,21		G
		Stratford, Baltinglass Street	21	RC	
		Chapel Street		Old RC	
		Church Street		EC	G
52	Rathdrum	Ballygannon	30		G
		Rathdrum, Main Street	30	EC M	G
53	Rathnew	Killoughter	25		G
		Town of Rathnew	25		G
		Wicklow, Church Street	25	EC	G
54	Rathsallagh				
55	Rathtoole	Ballycore	20		G
56	Redcross	Village of Redcross	35	EC	G
57	Tober	Tober Demesne	9,15		G

www.ingramcontent.com/pod-product-compliance
Lightning Source LLC
Chambersburg PA
CBHW081432270326
41932CB00019B/3171